Also by Eric Agyemang Duah

Mastering AI in Law

The AI Uprising

The AI Messiah

The Memory Traders

Sworn not to Love Again

PERFECT PROMPTING

A Practical Guide to Prompt Engineering for Innovative Professionals

Revised Edition

Eric Agyemang Duah

PromptTech
Consulting
and Publishing Services

Perfect Prompting: A Practical Guide to Prompt Engineering for Innovative Professionals

Revised Edition October 2025

ISBN: 979-8232961022

PromptTech
Consulting
and Publishing Services

To Adom Nyame,
for granting me the wisdom, knowledge, and understanding
to write this book—
a work that has become a blessing to many.

"For the Lord gives wisdom; from his mouth come knowledge and understanding."
—Proverbs 2:6 (NIV)

Contents

Preface

This book began with a question that resonates across professions: *How can we work intelligently with artificial intelligence?*

As a generative AI professional and author navigating the accelerating pace of digital transformation, I have witnessed a growing need for clear, practical, and ethically grounded guidance on using large language models such as ChatGPT, Gemini, Perplexity, and Copilot. These tools are not simply engines of automation, they are emerging collaborators in thinking, creativity, and problem solving.

That question naturally led to prompt engineering, the essential skill that shapes effective human and AI collaboration. Prompting is more than giving instructions, it is a structured way of thinking, asking better questions, and guiding systems toward meaningful and responsible outcomes.

The speed of advancement in AI demands continuous learning and adaptation. For this revised edition of *Perfect*

Prompting, the content has been comprehensively updated to reflect current platform capabilities, refined frameworks for greater clarity and consistency, and an expanded collection of more than 200 high value Prompt Packs. These updates ensure that the strategies in this book remain relevant, practical, and immediately applicable in today's professional landscape.

Perfect Prompting: A Practical Guide to Prompt Engineering for Innovative Professionals is written for professionals, educators, students, and lifelong learners who want to harness the power of AI while preserving the irreplaceable role of human judgment. This is not a general celebration of artificial intelligence. It is a structured and responsible guide to using it effectively and ethically.

The book is organized into four comprehensive parts: foundational AI concepts; core principles and techniques of prompting; practical use cases and tool evaluation; and extensive profession specific Prompt Packs designed for real world application.

Whether you are a software engineer refining code, a teacher personalizing instruction, or an architect exploring generative design, my hope is that this guide provides the clarity and confidence to make AI work with you, not just for you, and never in place of you.

Ultimately, this book affirms an enduring truth: even in an age of intelligent machines, progress is still defined by the quality of our questions, the clarity of our goals, and the strength of our values.

Eric Agyemang Duah
Author

Introduction

Artificial intelligence is rapidly reshaping the modern professional landscape. From automating complex tasks to uncovering new insights, AI tools have moved beyond futuristic concepts and become practical drivers of innovation, efficiency, and competitive advantage. Yet harnessing their full value requires more than access to the tools, it requires a clear understanding of prompt engineering, the discipline of communicating effectively with AI systems.

Perfect Prompting: A Practical Guide to Prompt Engineering for Innovative Professionals provides a multidisciplinary roadmap for navigating and thriving in this AI powered era. This revised edition has been fully updated to reflect recent platform developments and evolving best practices, ensuring you gain current, practical, and immediately applicable strategies. The book bridges the gap between AI's vast potential and its real world professional use.

The journey begins with Part I, *AI Fundamentals,* which establishes a clear foundation for understanding what artificial intelligence is and how it works. This section explores key elements, types of AI, and its transformative influence across industries. It also addresses ethical and societal considerations, offering a balanced and responsible perspective. Throughout this part, prompt engineering is introduced as the essential skill for turning AI capability into meaningful outcomes.

In Part II, *Prompt Engineering and Its Professional Applications,* the focus shifts to the craft that shapes successful human and AI interaction. You will learn the structure of effective prompts and explore techniques such as zero shot, few shot, and chain of thought prompting, along with iterative refinement and prompt chaining. This section also demonstrates how assigning clear roles to AI improves precision and relevance, highlights common prompting mistakes, and provides practical strategies to ensure your interactions remain focused and productive.

Building on these skills, Part III, A*I Tools and Their Effective Use Cases,* guides you through the rapidly expanding ecosystem of AI platforms. You will explore widely used tools including ChatGPT, Gemini, Suno, Canva AI, Microsoft Copilot, Midjourney, and Perplexity AI. This section shows how to integrate these tools into professional workflows, evaluate and select platforms strategically, understand their current limitations, and navigate the evolving regulatory environment.

The book culminates in Part IV, *Practical Prompt Packs for Professionals,* an extensive collection of targeted, ready to use prompts tailored to more than thirty professions. Whether you are summarizing complex documents, designing personalized learning materials, or developing strategic marketing content, this section provides structured prompt frameworks that translate directly into real world results.

Whether you are a professional expanding your capabilities, an educator bringing AI into the classroom, or a researcher examining AI's practical and ethical dimensions, *Perfect Prompting* equips you to work with AI confidently, precisely, and responsibly. The goal is not simply to use AI, but to use it well, with clarity of purpose and strength of judgment.

PART I

AI Fundamentals

Artificial Intelligence (AI) has transitioned from the realm of science fiction and academic theory into a transformative force shaping nearly every sector of modern society. From healthcare diagnostics and financial forecasting to autonomous vehicles and natural language processing, AI underpins many of today's most consequential technological advances. Understanding the core principles of AI is therefore essential not only for computer scientists and engineers, but also for educators, policymakers, business leaders, and professionals across a wide range of disciplines.

This chapter introduces foundational artificial intelligence concepts, offering a clear definition and establishing the groundwork for examining its types, underlying mechanisms, capabilities, and societal implications. By clarifying what artificial intelligence is and, critically, what it is not, readers are better equipped to evaluate its potential, limitations, and ethical considerations. Throughout this book, prompt engineering emerges as a central discipline for effectively harnessing artificial intelligence systems in professional and institutional contexts.

Defining Artificial Intelligence

Artificial intelligence is most commonly defined through the work of John McCarthy, a pioneering computer scientist and cognitive theorist widely regarded as one of the founding figures of the field. McCarthy was a professor at institutions such as Stanford University and the Massachusetts Institute of Technology (MIT), and he played a central role in shaping artificial intelligence as a formal area of scientific inquiry.

McCarthy coined the term *Artificial Intelligence* in 1955 and helped establish the discipline during the Dartmouth Summer Research Project on Artificial Intelligence in 1956, a landmark event that formally introduced artificial intelligence as a distinct research domain.

He later articulated the following definition:

> *"Artificial Intelligence is the science and engineering of making intelligent machines, especially intelligent computer programs."*
> *— John McCarthy*

This definition reflects McCarthy's intention to frame artificial intelligence as both a theoretical discipline and an applied engineering endeavor. Rather than restricting intelligence to human imitation, McCarthy emphasized the development of systems capable of exhibiting intelligent behavior, regardless of whether such systems mirror human cognitive processes.

In the original 1955–1956 Dartmouth proposal, McCarthy and his collaborators described artificial intelligence research as an effort to enable machines to use language, form abstractions, solve problems traditionally associated with human intelligence, and improve performance through experience. Although the proposal did not offer a single, formalized sentence definition, it established the conceptual foundations that later informed McCarthy's concise characterization of artificial intelligence as a scientific and engineering discipline.

Unlike traditional software systems that operate through explicitly programmed, rule-based instructions, modern artificial intelligence systems rely on statistical models, learning algorithms, and large-scale data processing to identify patterns and generate outputs with limited direct human intervention. A defining feature of such systems is their capacity to learn from data, allowing performance to improve iteratively as new information is encountered.

This framing remains central to contemporary artificial intelligence research and practice. It also provides the conceptual foundation for prompt engineering, which focuses on guiding intelligent systems through carefully structured inputs rather than through explicit procedural programming.

Mimicking Human Cognitive Functions

AI systems do not replicate the human brain, which operates through biological neural networks and consciousness-driven cognition. Instead, they rely on mathematical models, computational architectures, and algorithmic processes to approximate selected aspects of human cognitive behavior. By analyzing data, inferring relationships, and applying probabilistic reasoning or heuristics, AI systems can solve complex problems and, in narrowly defined tasks, often exceed human performance in speed, scale, and consistency.

For instance, AI-driven diagnostic systems have demonstrated high levels of accuracy in identifying diseases from medical imaging data, in some cases rivaling or surpassing expert clinicians under controlled conditions[3]. These achievements, however, reflect pattern recognition and statistical inference rather than genuine understanding.

It is therefore essential to emphasize that AI systems possess neither consciousness nor emotional awareness. They do not "understand" information in a human sense; instead, they generate outputs based on learned statistical regularities and probability distributions derived from training data[4].

The Evolution and Growth of AI

Since its formal emergence in the mid-twentieth century, AI has progressed through several distinct phases. Early research focused primarily on symbolic reasoning, logic-based representations, and rule-driven expert systems. Subsequent advances in machine learning shifted the paradigm toward data-driven approaches, enabling systems to improve performance through experience rather than explicit programming.

In recent decades, deep learning—a specialized subset of machine learning employing multi-layered neural networks—has driven significant breakthroughs across numerous domains. Technologies such as speech recognition, computer vision, autonomous navigation, and large-scale recommendation systems are largely powered by deep learning architectures[5].

Today, AI has evolved from an experimental academic pursuit into a foundational driver of innovation across industries including healthcare, finance, transportation, marketing, and education. The rapid acceleration of AI adoption reflects not only its technical maturity, but also its economic value and the substantial investments it attracts from governments, research institutions, and private enterprises worldwide.

This foundational understanding establishes the context for deeper exploration of AI's technical operations and, crucially, for mastering prompt engineering—the essential professional skill that enables humans to communicate effectively with AI systems and unlock their full practical potential.

Key Elements of AI

At the core of the significant advances in Artificial Intelligence (AI) lie several foundational elements that enable machines to perform increasingly complex, adaptive, and context-aware tasks. These key components—Machine Learning, Natural Language Processing, Computer Vision, and Robotics—constitute the technical pillars of modern AI and serve as the primary drivers of its rapid adoption across professional, industrial, and social domains.

Machine Learning

Machine Learning (ML) is a central component of AI that enables systems to learn from data and improve performance without being explicitly programmed for each task. ML relies on statistical models and computational algorithms to identify patterns, draw inferences, and generate predictions or decisions based on historical or real-time data inputs[1].

Machine learning approaches are commonly categorized into three principal types:

- **Supervised learning:** Systems are trained using labeled datasets in which each input is paired with a known output. This approach is widely used in applications such as email spam detection, image classification, and medical diagnosis.

- **Unsupervised learning:** Systems analyze unlabeled data to discover underlying structures, relationships, or patterns without predefined outcomes. Common use cases include customer segmentation, anomaly detection, and topic modeling.

- **Reinforcement learning:** An agent learns through interaction with an environment, receiving rewards or penalties that guide behavior toward optimal outcomes over time. This approach underpins many advances in game-playing systems, robotics, and autonomous driving.

Machine learning powers a broad range of everyday technologies, including recommendation systems, predictive text input, fraud detection, and diagnostic decision support tools in healthcare.

Natural Language Processing

Natural Language Processing (NLP) enables AI systems to understand, interpret, generate, and respond to human language in meaningful and context-sensitive ways. This capability allows machines to engage in dialogue, perform translation, analyze sentiment, summarize content, extract information, and generate code or structured text[2].

Applications such as conversational agents, voice assistants, and large language models rely heavily on NLP techniques to process spoken or written language. In enterprise and institutional settings, NLP is used for sentiment analysis, customer feedback monitoring, document classification, and knowledge extraction from large textual datasets. In healthcare, NLP techniques support the analysis of clinical notes and medical records.

NLP integrates insights from linguistics with machine learning and deep learning methods to model grammar, semantics, context, and intent—enabling systems to move beyond keyword matching toward more nuanced language understanding.

Computer Vision

Computer Vision enables machines to perceive, interpret, and analyze visual data, including images and video streams. Using techniques such as convolutional neural networks and other deep learning architectures, computer vision systems can recognize objects, classify images, detect faces, interpret scenes, and analyze complex visual patterns[3].

This capability is widely applied across multiple sectors, including:

- **Security**: Facial recognition, access control, and video surveillance systems.
- **Retail**: Automated inventory monitoring, shelf analytics, and customer behavior analysis.
- **Healthcare**: Detection and assessment of medical conditions through radiographic and imaging analysis.

By approximating aspects of human visual perception through computational means, computer vision enables AI systems to interact more effectively with the physical and visual world.

Robotics

Robotics combines AI with mechanical and electronic systems to create autonomous or semi-autonomous machines capable of performing tasks in real-world environments. AI-enabled robots can navigate complex spaces, manipulate objects, adapt to changing conditions, and operate with limited human supervision[4].

In manufacturing, intelligent robots perform precision assembly and quality control. In healthcare, robotic systems assist clinicians in minimally invasive surgical procedures. In logistics and warehousing, autonomous robots optimize inventory management and order fulfillment.

Modern robotic systems integrate data from multiple sensors—including cameras, LiDAR, inertial measurement units, and tactile sensors—which AI algorithms process to perceive the environment and guide decision-making in real time.

Collectively, these key elements form the foundational architecture of contemporary AI systems. Together, they enable machines to learn, reason, perceive, communicate, and act—fundamentally reshaping professional workflows, organizational decision-making, and value creation in the digital economy.

Types of AI

In the rapidly evolving field of Artificial Intelligence, understanding the major categories of AI is essential for professionals seeking to apply these technologies responsibly and effectively. AI systems are commonly classified into three broad types based on their capability, scope, and degree of autonomy: Artificial Narrow Intelligence (ANI), Artificial General Intelligence (AGI), and Artificial Superintelligence (ASI). These categories reflect an AI system's capacity for generalization, adaptability, and performance beyond its original training objectives.

Artificial Narrow Intelligence (ANI)

Artificial Narrow Intelligence, often referred to as *Narrow AI* or *Weak AI*, encompasses systems designed to perform specific tasks within well-defined domains. These systems operate with high efficiency and accuracy but lack the ability to generalize knowledge or reasoning beyond their trained scope without substantial retraining or human intervention[1].

Although ANI systems do not exhibit human-like understanding or broad reasoning abilities, they excel at specialized tasks and are deeply embedded in contemporary professional, industrial, and consumer technologies.

Representative examples include:

- **Large Language Models (LLMs):** Systems such as ChatGPT, Gemini, Microsoft Copilot, Perplexity, Meta's LLaMA, and DeepSeek generate text or multimodal outputs in response to prompts. Despite architectural differences, they are optimized for specific tasks such as language modeling and content generation rather than generalized intelligence.

- **Recommendation Systems:** Platforms such as Spotify and Amazon personalize content and product suggestions based on user behavior and historical data.

- **Facial Recognition Software:** Technologies including Apple Face ID, Clearview AI, and Amazon Rekognition are used for identity verification, surveillance, and security applications.

- **Healthcare Diagnostic Tools:** Systems such as Google DeepMind's AlphaFold for protein structure prediction, IBM Watson Health, and AI-driven medical imaging platforms assist clinicians in diagnostic decision-making.

- **Fraud Detection Algorithms:** Financial services deploy systems such as Mastercard's Decision Intelligence, PayPal's fraud prevention engine, and Stripe Radar to identify anomalous transaction patterns in real time.

- **Voice Assistants:** Applications such as Siri, Alexa, and Google Assistant respond to voice commands within constrained functional domains.

While Narrow AI systems support many professional workflows—particularly in customer service, diagnostics, content generation, and financial analysis—they do not possess independent reasoning, emotional awareness, or the capacity to transfer knowledge across unrelated domains.

Artificial General Intelligence (AGI)

Artificial General Intelligence (AGI), sometimes referred to as *Strong AI*, denotes a hypothetical form of intelligence capable of human-level understanding and adaptability across a broad range of tasks. An AGI system would be able to perform any intellectual activity that a human can, including reasoning, learning, creativity, ethical judgment, and complex problem-solving[1].

Unlike ANI, AGI would generalize knowledge across domains, learn efficiently from limited data, adapt to novel situations, and improve its capabilities autonomously. Such systems would exhibit contextual awareness and flexible reasoning rather than task-specific optimization.

Key characteristics commonly associated with AGI include:

- **Cross-Domain Learning:** The ability to transfer knowledge and skills across unrelated fields.
- **Abstraction and Reasoning:** Understanding abstract concepts such as strategy, causality, and ethical principles.
- **Contextual Awareness:** Sensitivity to situational, cultural, and social nuances.
- **Creativity:** Generation of novel ideas, solutions, or artistic expressions.
- **Emotional and Social Intelligence:** Interpretation of and appropriate response to human emotions.

- **Common-Sense Reasoning:** Practical understanding of everyday cause-and-effect relationships.

Potential Benefits of AGI

If developed safely and aligned with human values, AGI could offer transformative benefits, including:

- **Accelerated Scientific Discovery:** Autonomous hypothesis generation, experimental design, and large-scale data analysis across disciplines such as medicine, climate science, and physics[2].

- **Personalized Education and Healthcare:** Adaptive tutoring systems and individualized treatment planning delivered in real time[3].

- **Cross-Disciplinary Innovation:** Solutions to complex global challenges such as pandemics, clean energy development, and poverty reduction.

- **Human-AI Collaboration:** Augmented creativity and strategic decision-making in policy, architecture, engineering, and the arts.

- **Advanced Automation:** Automation of complex cognitive tasks that require judgment, reasoning, and contextual understanding[4].

Current Status and Research Directions

Despite significant advances in large language models and multimodal AI systems, no existing technology qualifies as AGI. Current systems—including ChatGPT, Gemini, and Perplexity—remain forms of Narrow AI, lacking generalized reasoning, autonomous learning, and genuine understanding[5].

Ongoing AGI research focuses on areas such as:

- Multimodal learning (integrating text, images, audio, and video)
- Meta-learning (learning how to learn)
- Self-supervised learning (reducing dependence on labeled datasets)
- Human-in-the-loop safety and alignment mechanisms

Predictions regarding the timeline for AGI development vary widely, with estimates ranging from decades to longer horizons. Many researchers emphasize caution, highlighting unresolved safety, ethical, and governance challenges[6].

Artificial Superintelligence (ASI)

Artificial Superintelligence (ASI) refers to a hypothetical form of intelligence that would surpass human cognitive abilities across all domains, including reasoning, creativity, emotional intelligence, and decision-making[3]. An ASI system would likely be capable of rapid self-improvement, potentially leading to exponential increases in capability.

Potential benefits of ASI are often theorized to include:

- Solutions to global challenges such as climate change, pandemics, and energy scarcity.
- Transformative advances in science, medicine, economics, and education.
- Accelerated progress in areas such as space exploration, biotechnology, and global governance.

At the same time, ASI raises profound ethical, safety, and existential concerns. Without robust alignment to human values and effective control mechanisms, superintelligent systems could behave in unpredictable or harmful ways[4]. Although ASI remains speculative, it motivates active research in AI alignment, safety, and long-term governance.

Summary Table 1.1: AI Categories

AI Type	Description	Current Status	Examples	Key Traits
Artificial Narrow Intelligence (ANI)	Specialized, task specific intelligence	Actively deployed	ChatGPT, Siri, Face ID, Netflix Recommender	Fast, domain-specific, non-adaptive
Artificial General Intelligence (AGI)	Broad, human-level cognitive abilities	Not yet achieved (theoretical)	N/A	Adaptable, cross-domain, human-level cognition
Artificial Superintelligence (ASI)	Intelligence surpassing humans in all areas	Entirely theoretical	N/A	Autonomous, self-improving, exponential intelligence

Conclusion

As summarized in Table 1.1, understanding these categories of AI is essential for prompt engineers and professionals who engage with AI systems on a daily basis. Today's leading applications—such as ChatGPT and Gemini—are highly advanced forms of Artificial Narrow Intelligence that simulate understanding without possessing genuine comprehension or general intelligence.

Distinguishing between ANI, AGI, and ASI enables practitioners to set realistic expectations, apply AI tools more effectively, and anticipate future developments responsibly. As AI capabilities continue to evolve, prompt engineering will remain a critical skill—beginning with mastery of Narrow AI systems and extending toward effective human–AI collaboration in increasingly complex and autonomous environments. Ethical foresight, safety alignment, and sound governance will be indispensable in shaping AI's long-term impact.

Transforming Industries with AI

Artificial Intelligence is no longer a peripheral innovation, it has become a core transformative force across nearly every sector of the global economy. As AI matures, it enables professionals and organizations to reimagine workflows, improve decision making, enhance efficiency, and create new forms of value. Whether in medicine, finance, education, manufacturing, or media, AI is being woven into the fabric of how modern industries operate and evolve[1].

Healthcare

In healthcare, AI is driving a shift from reactive treatment to proactive, data-informed care. AI-powered diagnostic systems analyze medical images such as X-rays, MRIs, and dermatological scans with levels of accuracy that in certain tasks rival those of trained specialists. These systems help detect conditions such as cancer, fractures, and cardiovascular abnormalities more quickly, reducing the time between diagnosis and intervention[2].

Beyond diagnostics, AI supports clinical decision making by identifying patterns in electronic health records and assisting in predicting patient outcomes. In operating rooms, AI-assisted surgical technologies enhance precision, supporting safer minimally invasive procedures. Natural language processing tools streamline documentation by transcribing physician notes, extracting clinical terminology, and organizing patient records. Drug discovery, once a lengthy and costly process, is being accelerated by AI systems that analyze molecular structures and identify promising compounds for further research.

Finance

The finance industry has long relied on data analysis, but AI has significantly expanded the scale and sophistication of these capabilities. AI plays a central role in fraud detection systems, monitoring transactions in real time and flagging unusual patterns that may indicate fraudulent activity. These systems continuously learn from new data, adapting to emerging threats[3].

Investment firms employ AI in algorithmic trading, where models make rapid buy or sell decisions based on live market signals. In retail banking and financial technology platforms, AI supports intelligent customer service through virtual assistants and enhances credit assessment by analyzing broader data sources. AI-driven risk analysis tools also help financial institutions evaluate exposure and navigate regulatory requirements in volatile markets.

Education

AI is reshaping education by personalizing learning experiences and improving institutional efficiency. Intelligent tutoring systems use machine learning to adapt lessons in real time, aligning instruction with each student's pace, strengths, and challenges. These platforms deliver targeted feedback and customized study pathways, supporting more effective learning outcomes[4].

Educators benefit from AI-assisted grading tools that handle routine assessments, allowing more time for meaningful student engagement. AI systems can also identify students at risk of falling behind by analyzing participation patterns, performance trends, and attendance data. Administrators use AI to streamline scheduling, enrollment management, and resource planning, making educational institutions more responsive and efficient.

Manufacturing and Supply Chain

In manufacturing, AI supports the shift toward smarter, more resilient production environments. Predictive maintenance systems rely on sensor data to detect anomalies and forecast equipment failures before they occur. This reduces downtime, lowers maintenance costs, and extends the lifespan of critical machinery[5].

Computer vision technologies enhance quality control by identifying defects or inconsistencies in real time. In supply chain management, AI improves demand forecasting by analyzing historical sales, seasonal patterns, and market dynamics. This supports more accurate production planning and reduces waste. AI-enabled robotics further strengthen automation by performing complex physical tasks in warehouses, assembly lines, and distribution centers with high speed and precision.

Retail and E-Commerce

Retailers increasingly use AI to deliver personalized shopping experiences and optimize operations. Recommendation systems analyze customer behavior, including browsing history and purchasing patterns, to suggest relevant products. This personalization improves customer satisfaction, conversion rates, and brand loyalty[6].

AI also supports dynamic pricing strategies, adjusting prices in response to demand, competitor activity, and inventory levels. Customer service benefits from AI-powered virtual assistants that handle inquiries, process returns, and guide purchasing decisions. Behind the scenes, AI enhances inventory management by forecasting stock requirements and recommending replenishment schedules. Visual search tools allow shoppers to upload images and find similar products, connecting inspiration directly to purchase.

Transportation and Logistics

Transportation is undergoing significant transformation with AI improving safety, efficiency, and coordination. Autonomous and semi-autonomous vehicles use AI to interpret data from cameras, sensors, and navigation systems, enabling real-time driving decisions. These systems assess traffic patterns, road conditions, and pedestrian behavior to support safer mobility solutions[7].

In logistics, AI-driven routing systems determine efficient delivery paths based on traffic, weather, and operational constraints. Predictive analytics help organizations anticipate delays and adjust schedules proactively. At ports, airports, and distribution hubs, AI coordinates human workers and automated systems to streamline cargo movement and reduce bottlenecks.

Entertainment and Media

In entertainment and media, AI is influencing both content creation and consumption. Streaming platforms use AI to analyze user preferences and recommend films, shows, and music that align with individual tastes. These systems continually refine personalization based on viewing and listening behavior[8].

AI also assists in creative production. Musicians, filmmakers, designers, and writers use AI tools to co-generate music, scripts, visual art, and video elements. In post-production, AI automates editing tasks, enhances visual effects, and supports voice and facial animation for localization. News organizations use AI to generate summaries, analyze large data sets, and produce visualizations. Marketing teams apply AI to evaluate audience sentiment and tailor campaigns to specific audience segments.

Conclusion

Artificial Intelligence is transforming industries by redefining processes, empowering professionals, and unlocking new levels of efficiency and innovation. Its adoption is no longer a question of possibility, but of strategy and responsibility. Organizations and professionals who understand how to integrate AI thoughtfully will help shape the future of their fields. As this transformation continues, AI must be developed and applied with strategic foresight, ethical consideration, and a commitment to enhancing human capability rather than replacing it.

Ethical and Societal Challenges in AI

As artificial intelligence becomes increasingly integrated into decision making systems, public services, and organizational infrastructures, its societal implications grow more complex and urgent. While AI offers transformative potential, it also raises serious ethical concerns that professionals, developers, regulators, and users must address. Understanding these challenges is essential to ensure that AI development and use align with human values, rights, and dignity[1].

Bias and Discrimination

One of the most pressing ethical challenges in AI is bias, both in training data and in algorithm design. AI systems learn from historical data, and if that data reflects racial, gender-based, socioeconomic, or cultural biases, AI systems may reproduce or amplify those patterns in their outputs[2].

For example, AI-driven hiring tools have shown preference for certain demographics due to biased training datasets. Facial recognition technologies have demonstrated higher error rates for people with darker skin tones, reflecting imbalanced data representation. In the legal system, algorithmic risk assessment tools have disproportionately affected marginalized groups. These outcomes are not merely technical flaws, they mirror the social conditions in which AI systems are developed.

Prompt engineering can help reduce bias by guiding models with carefully structured, context-aware prompts. By refining instructions and encouraging inclusive framing, professionals can reduce unfair representations and promote more equitable AI-assisted decisions.

Privacy and Surveillance

AI systems depend on vast quantities of personal data, raising significant privacy concerns. Whether used for targeted advertising, personalized recommendations, or behavioral prediction, the collection and processing of personal information present risks related to consent, ownership, and surveillance[3].

Governments and corporations increasingly deploy AI to monitor user behavior, collect biometric data, and analyze digital activity. In some regions, AI-enabled surveillance systems track citizens' movements and interactions with limited oversight, increasing the risk of civil liberties violations, social manipulation, and diminished personal autonomy.

Professionals using AI tools must remain vigilant about data sources, storage practices, and consent mechanisms to ensure responsible use.

Transparency and Explainability

Many AI systems, particularly those based on deep learning, operate as opaque systems that generate results without clear explanations. This lack of transparency is especially concerning in high-stakes fields such as healthcare, finance, and criminal justice, where stakeholders must understand how decisions are made[4].

Thoughtful prompt design can improve transparency by asking AI systems to explain reasoning steps, outline assumptions, or provide sources. While this does not fully solve technical opacity, it supports better human oversight and informed evaluation.

Explainable AI is an active area of research aimed at improving interpretability. Despite progress, a gap remains between technical model complexity and end-user understanding. Without sufficient transparency, trust weakens and accountability becomes difficult to establish.

Job Insecurity and Economic Inequality

AI is expected to create new roles while automating many existing tasks, particularly those involving routine or mid-skilled work. Industries such as manufacturing, transportation, and customer service already face workforce restructuring[5]. This shift may widen economic inequality, as highly skilled professionals benefit from AI integration while others face job displacement.

AI should be implemented in ways that augment human capabilities rather than fully replace workers. Prompt-driven workflows can support collaboration between humans and AI, enabling upskilling and productivity enhancement. Without robust reskilling initiatives, inclusive economic strategies, and social safety nets, AI adoption risks deepening income disparities.

Autonomy, Control, and Responsibility

As AI systems gain greater autonomy, questions of accountability become more urgent. Determining responsibility when an autonomous vehicle causes an accident or when an AI system denies a loan can be complex. Responsibility may be distributed among developers, deployers, and users, creating legal and ethical uncertainty[6].

In prompt engineering, incorporating checkpoints, constraints, and human review stages helps maintain oversight. Human-in-the-loop frameworks, clear liability guidelines, and continuous monitoring are necessary to ensure that automated systems remain under meaningful human control.

Global Inequity and AI Access

AI research and infrastructure are concentrated in a limited number of countries and corporations, while many developing regions face barriers related to connectivity, resources, and technical capacity[7]. This imbalance risks widening global disparities in innovation and economic opportunity.

Inclusive AI development and prompt design practices that reflect diverse languages, cultures, and social contexts can make AI systems more globally relevant. Without such inclusion, AI technologies may reinforce cultural dominance and exclude underrepresented populations.

Regulation and Governance

Legal and regulatory systems struggle to keep pace with rapid AI advancement, leaving unresolved issues concerning data protection, fairness, intellectual property, and accountability[8]. Initiatives such as the European Union Artificial Intelligence Act and international ethical guidelines represent meaningful progress, yet governance must remain adaptive and globally coordinated.

Effective AI oversight requires collaboration among policymakers, technologists, ethicists, industry leaders, and civil society. Regulation should balance innovation with protection of public interests and fundamental rights.

AI Alignment and Long-Term Safety

As AI systems become more capable and autonomous, long-term safety and alignment concerns grow. Systems that are not properly aligned with human intentions may produce harmful or unintended outcomes. These risks arise not only from speculative future systems but also from present-day models that behave unpredictably due to poorly defined objectives or ambiguous prompts[9].

Prompt engineering plays a foundational role in alignment by clearly communicating goals, constraints, and values. Alignment research aims to develop systems that respect human preferences, avoid manipulation, and defer appropriately to human judgment. As AI capabilities expand, alignment remains both a technical challenge and an ethical imperative.

The Human Role in the AI Age

AI remains a human-created tool shaped by human decisions. Ensuring that it serves humanity requires continuous reflection, interdisciplinary dialogue, and active professional responsibility. The central question is not only what AI can do, but what it should do, and who determines those boundaries.

Conclusion

As AI continues to transform society, ethical awareness is no longer optional, it is a professional responsibility. The true measure of progress lies not in the intelligence of machines, but in the wisdom guiding their use. Whether designing systems, writing prompts, or adopting AI tools, professionals play a crucial role in shaping outcomes that uphold dignity, fairness, and justice. The future of AI is both technical and ethical, and it must remain human-centered by design.

How AI Works

While AI may appear almost magical in its ability to generate human-like text, diagnosing diseases, or drive autonomous vehicles, its underlying mechanisms are grounded in structured computation, mathematics, and data. Understanding how AI works enables professionals to engage with these systems more critically, apply them responsibly, and recognize both their capabilities and their limitations. At the core of all AI systems are algorithms, data, models, and a process broadly referred to as learning.

Data: The Lifeblood of AI

All AI systems begin with data. Data provides the raw material from which AI models learn patterns, infer relationships, and generate outputs. Depending on the application, data may be structured, such as spreadsheets or relational databases, semi-structured, such as JSON or XML files, or unstructured, including text, images, audio, and video. The quality, quantity, diversity, and representativeness of data directly influence an AI system's accuracy, robustness, and fairness[1].

For example, a language model such as ChatGPT is trained on large collections of text drawn from books, academic literature, public web content, and other written sources in order to learn statistical patterns of language. In contrast, a medical diagnostic system is typically trained on labeled datasets, such as X-rays or CT scans, paired with clinical annotations identifying known conditions. In both cases, the system learns associations within the data rather than acquiring understanding in a human sense.

Algorithms and Models: The Engines of Intelligence

An algorithm is a defined sequence of computational steps designed to solve a problem or perform a task. In AI systems, algorithms process data, evaluate outcomes, and iteratively update models. A model is the resulting mathematical representation produced when an algorithm has been trained on data.

In supervised learning, a model is trained using datasets that pair inputs with known outputs. The algorithm adjusts the model's internal parameters to minimize the difference between predicted and actual outcomes, a process known as optimization. Over repeated iterations, the model improves its performance by reducing error.

In unsupervised learning, algorithms identify patterns, groupings, or latent structures within data without labeled outcomes. Models vary widely in complexity, ranging from simple linear statistical techniques to deep neural networks capable of learning highly abstract representations[2].

Machine Learning: Learning from Experience

While the previous chapter introduced Machine Learning as a core component of Artificial Intelligence (*see page 7*), this section examines how learning occurs in practice and how models improve through data-driven feedback.

Machine Learning (ML) is the primary mechanism through which AI systems adapt and improve over time. Rather than relying on rigid, hand-coded rules, ML systems generalize from examples, enabling them to make predictions or decisions when presented with new data[3].

The core approaches to machine learning include:

- **Supervised Learning:** Models learn from labeled datasets, such as email classification systems trained on messages labeled as spam or not spam.
- **Unsupervised Learning:** Models analyze unlabeled data to uncover patterns or clusters, commonly used in customer segmentation and anomaly detection.

- **Reinforcement Learning:** Agents learn by interacting with an environment and receiving feedback in the form of rewards or penalties. This approach underpins many advances in robotics, game-playing systems, and autonomous control.

Through iterative feedback loops, often implemented using optimization techniques such as gradient descent, models progressively refine their internal parameters to improve accuracy and decision quality.

Deep Learning and Neural Networks

Deep learning is a specialized subset of machine learning that employs artificial neural networks composed of multiple layers, commonly referred to as deep neural networks. These layered architectures enable systems to learn hierarchical and abstract representations directly from raw data[4].

In image recognition tasks, early layers detect basic features such as edges or textures, while deeper layers identify higher-level structures such as faces or objects. In natural language processing, deep learning models capture relationships among words, sentence structure, and semantic context.

Widely used deep learning architectures include:

- **Convolutional Neural Networks (CNNs):** Optimized for image and video analysis.

- **Recurrent Neural Networks (RNNs):** Designed for sequential data such as speech, handwriting, or time-series signals.

- **Transformers:** The architecture underlying modern large language models such as ChatGPT and Gemini. Transformers use attention mechanisms to model contextual relationships across entire sequences, enabling advanced capabilities in translation, summarization, and reasoning[5].

Training vs. Inference

AI systems typically operate in two distinct phases, training and inference.

During training, a model is exposed to large datasets and iteratively adjusts its internal parameters to learn patterns and relationships. This phase is computationally intensive and commonly relies on specialized hardware such as Graphics Processing Units and Tensor Processing Units. GPUs excel at performing parallel mathematical operations, while TPUs, custom accelerators developed by

Google, are optimized for machine learning workloads, particularly in deep learning frameworks.

Once training is complete, the system enters the inference phase. During inference, the trained model applies its learned parameters to generate predictions, classifications, or responses based on new inputs. For example, when a user submits a prompt to ChatGPT, the model performs inference to generate a contextually appropriate response in real time[6].

Limitations of Current AI Systems

Despite their sophistication, contemporary AI systems have fundamental limitations. They do not possess consciousness, self-awareness, intent, or genuine understanding. Their outputs are constrained by the scope, quality, and biases present in their training data. As a result, AI systems may produce inaccurate, misleading, or biased outputs, particularly when confronted with ambiguous, adversarial, or unfamiliar inputs[7].

Many advanced AI models also require substantial computational resources and large datasets. These requirements raise concerns related to accessibility, environmental sustainability, data privacy, and fairness. Such limitations underscore the importance of responsible design, deployment, and governance.

Human-AI Collaboration

AI systems do not replace human intelligence. Instead, they augment human capabilities by automating repetitive, data-intensive, or high-speed tasks. This allows professionals to focus on judgment, creativity, ethical reasoning, and interpersonal engagement.

In fields such as medicine, law, education, design, and content creation, AI increasingly functions as a collaborative partner rather than a substitute. Understanding how AI works equips professionals to use these tools thoughtfully, interpret outputs critically, and integrate them effectively into human-centered workflows.

Understanding the operational foundations of AI is therefore not merely a technical exercise. It is an essential competency for navigating the modern digital economy with insight, responsibility, and confidence.

Prompt Engineering and its Professional Applications

PART II

Prompt engineering has emerged as one of the most essential digital literacy skills in the age of Artificial Intelligence. As large language models such as ChatGPT, Perplexity, Gemini, and similar systems become embedded in professional workflows, the ability to craft precise, purposeful, and context-aware prompts has become a vital competency. Prompt engineering extends beyond merely interacting with an AI system. It represents a structured and strategic form of communication designed to maximize usefulness, accuracy, and alignment with intended professional outcomes.

What is Prompt Engineering?

Prompt engineering is the art and science of formulating inputs, commonly referred to as prompts, that guide an Artificial Intelligence model toward producing high-quality, relevant, and reliable outputs. It involves defining clear instructions, establishing appropriate context, specifying tone or format requirements, and iterating based on observed results. A well-engineered prompt functions simultaneously as a query and a framework, enabling the AI system to interpret user intent with greater precision[1].

In professional settings, prompt design directly influences the depth, accuracy, and direction of AI-generated responses. Understanding how different prompt structures shape reasoning and output allows professionals to engage AI as a cognitive assistant rather than as a passive automation tool.

The sections below outline five core categories of prompts, each accompanied by practical use cases that demonstrate their relevance across professional domains.

1. Task-Oriented Prompts

Task-oriented prompts instruct the AI to perform a specific and clearly defined action, such as summarizing documents, drafting correspondence, translating text, or revising content for clarity or tone. These prompts emphasize precision, constraints, and expected deliverables, making them well suited for administrative, procedural, and documentation-focused tasks.

Example Prompt

"Draft a two-paragraph executive summary of the attached quarterly marketing report, highlighting performance metrics and campaign effectiveness. The summary should be written in a professional tone for internal stakeholders."

This prompt clearly specifies the task, scope, tone, and audience. It directs the AI to extract relevant insights, organize information logically, and present the content concisely. Task-oriented prompts are widely used in legal, medical, administrative, and communications contexts, where accuracy and clarity are essential.

2. Creative Prompts

Creative prompts encourage the AI to generate original content, explore alternative perspectives, or produce stylistically expressive output. These prompts are typically open-ended within defined constraints and are used in storytelling, branding, marketing, education, and ideation workflows.

Example Prompt

"Write a short promotional script for a 30-second radio advertisement promoting a new eco-friendly electric bike brand. The tone should be energetic, youthful, and centered on sustainability."

This prompt establishes a creative objective while maintaining stylistic boundaries. The AI is expected to generate persuasive language that captures attention and conveys brand identity. Creative prompts enable professionals to accelerate content development while maintaining control over voice, tone, and messaging.

3. Problem-Solving Prompts

Problem-solving prompts guide the AI through structured analysis of real-world challenges. They require the system to identify potential causes, apply logical reasoning, and propose actionable solutions.

> ***Example Prompt***
>
> *"You are an operations consultant. A logistics company has experienced a 22 percent increase in delayed deliveries over the past quarter. Analyze possible causes of the delays and propose three solutions to improve delivery speed and reliability."*

By defining a professional role, presenting a measurable problem, and specifying an expected output, this prompt encourages analytical reasoning and solution-oriented thinking. Problem-solving prompts are particularly valuable in strategy, operations, engineering, supply chain management, and information technology contexts.

4. Conversational Prompts

Conversational prompts are designed to create interactive, dialogue-based exchanges that simulate human communication. These prompts are often role-based and are used for coaching, training, customer support simulations, and interpersonal skill development.

> ***Example Prompt***
>
> *"Act as a professional leadership coach. Begin a coaching conversation with a mid-level manager who is struggling to provide constructive feedback to their team. Use a supportive and inquisitive tone, and ask reflective questions."*

This prompt defines persona, audience, and interaction style. It elicits responses aimed at dialogue and reflection rather than information delivery alone. Conversational prompts are commonly used in human resources, leadership development, education, and customer experience training.

5. Analytical Prompts

Analytical prompts require the AI to evaluate complex information, synthesize multiple perspectives, and provide evidence-based conclusions or recommendations. These prompts often involve structured data, comparative evaluation, or interpretive judgment.

> ***Example Prompt***
>
> *"Analyze the company's quarterly financial reports and summarize key performance indicators, potential risks, and recommendations for improving profitability. Include a comparison with industry benchmarks and discuss factors influencing performance."*

This prompt directs the AI to interpret data, identify trends, benchmark outcomes, and produce insight-driven analysis. Analytical prompts are particularly relevant in finance, research, journalism, policy analysis, and business intelligence environments.

Conclusion

Each prompt category represents a distinct mode of cognitive engagement, including directive execution, creative generation, logical reasoning, interpersonal interaction, and evaluative analysis. Professionals who align their objectives with the appropriate prompt structure can leverage Artificial Intelligence more effectively as a collaborative partner. Mastery of prompt engineering transforms AI interaction from a mechanical exercise into a strategic professional capability that enhances efficiency, insight, and decision-making.

The Significance of Prompts in Artificial Intelligence

Prompts are the initial inputs or instructions provided to Artificial Intelligence systems, particularly large language models, that shape and constrain their outputs. They encode a user's intent, contextual assumptions, tone, and objectives in natural language form.

In this capacity, prompts function as the primary interface between human cognition and machine-generated output. As Artificial Intelligence becomes increasingly embedded in professional, institutional, and creative workflows, the design of effective prompts has emerged as a decisive factor influencing system performance, reliability, and ethical use.

This chapter examines the significance of prompts not only from a technical perspective but also from practical, strategic, and ethical standpoints.

Guiding AI Systems

At a foundational level, prompts guide the behavior of an Artificial Intelligence model. They define the task to be performed, delimit the scope of the response, and specify expectations regarding tone, format, or level of detail. A well-constructed prompt does more than issue an instruction; it shapes how the system processes the request, despite the model's lack of genuine understanding or intent.

In high-stakes professional contexts such as medical analysis, legal review, or financial assessment, imprecise or poorly structured prompts can result in misleading, incomplete, or erroneous outputs. Conversely, prompts that clearly articulate role, purpose, and constraints enable closer alignment between human intention and machine-generated results.

For example, the prompt:

"Generate a summary of this patient's lab results."

is open-ended and susceptible to multiple interpretations, increasing the risk of omission or misrepresentation.

By contrast, the prompt:

> *"As a medical assistant, summarize this blood panel for a primary care physician. Highlight abnormal values and suggest possible causes, using medical terminology appropriate for a clinical note."*

clarifies role, audience, purpose, and content priorities. This added structure anchors the output within a human-defined interpretive framework, thereby reducing ambiguity and increasing practical usefulness.

Enabling Diverse Applications

One of the defining strengths of contemporary Artificial Intelligence systems lies in their adaptability across domains. A single model can support tasks ranging from software development and legal analysis to marketing communication and personalized education, provided it is guided by an appropriately designed prompt.

Prompts may take different forms, including task-oriented, creative, analytical, and conversational structures, each of which channels the model's behavior toward specific objectives. These categories, examined in detail in the preceding chapter, demonstrate how prompt engineering enables the effective deployment of AI systems across varied professional contexts, including education, healthcare, policy analysis, entertainment, and product development.

This versatility highlights the growing professional importance of prompt literacy. The ability to frame questions and tasks with clarity and intention increasingly determines whether Artificial Intelligence functions as a superficial convenience or as a meaningful cognitive partner.

Facilitating Human-AI Interaction

Beyond task execution, prompts play a central role in shaping human–AI collaboration. Rather than merely eliciting isolated answers, well-designed prompts support iterative, dialogic interaction in which AI assists, refines, extends, or accelerates human work.

This collaborative dynamic is particularly evident in fields where human judgment and contextual awareness remain essential:

- In healthcare, clinicians use prompts to draft clinical notes, summarize patient histories, or generate preliminary reports, reducing administrative burden while maintaining professional oversight.
- In education, instructors prompt AI tutors to deliver personalized explanations, practice exercises, or formative feedback tailored to individual learners.

- In business and management, professionals employ prompts to rehearse negotiations, explore strategic options, or prepare internal communications.

In each case, the prompt mediates clarity, collaboration, and control. When carefully constructed, it allows humans to retain agency while benefiting from the scale, speed, and pattern recognition capabilities of Artificial Intelligence systems.

Enhancing AI Performance

Although considerable attention is often devoted to the sophistication of AI models themselves, it is essential to recognize that even the most advanced systems are highly sensitive to how tasks are framed. Identical models can generate outputs that range from accurate and insightful to vague or unreliable, depending entirely on the prompt provided.

Effective prompts reduce ambiguity, constrain unwanted speculation, and steer outputs toward contextually appropriate results. This function is particularly critical in professional environments where AI-generated content influences decision-making, public communication, or published materials.

Consider the prompt:

> *"Write a news brief on the GDP growth rate for Q3."*

This instruction leaves key variables undefined, including geographic scope, data source, tone, and comparative context.

A more precise alternative:

> *"Draft a 150-word business news summary on the 2025 third-quarter United States GDP growth data, using verified figures from the Bureau of Economic Analysis. Include a comparison with the previous quarter and maintain a neutral, informative tone."*

By specifying length, source, scope, and stylistic expectations, the revised prompt significantly improves accuracy, relevance, and trustworthiness. In this sense, well-designed prompts function as performance multipliers, enhancing efficiency while mitigating risk.

Advancing AI Research

Prompts also occupy a central role in Artificial Intelligence research and evaluation. Researchers rely on carefully structured prompts to assess model capabilities, limitations, and behavioral tendencies. Common research applications include:

- Evaluating reasoning, coherence, and factual consistency
- Investigating bias and sensitivity to linguistic variation
- Benchmarking performance in zero-shot and few-shot learning scenarios

Entire research directions, such as prompt-based learning and instruction tuning, focus on how models respond to structured instructions and how such responses can be improved through training and fine-tuning.

Recent advances in prompting strategies, including chain-of-thought prompting and self-reflective prompting, have demonstrated new methods for eliciting improved reasoning transparency and structured problem-solving. As discussed later in the chapter on Advanced Prompting Techniques, approaches such as zero-shot, few-shot, and chain-of-thought prompting are significant both for practical application and for advancing theoretical understanding of large language models.

Accordingly, prompts should be understood not merely as tools for using Artificial Intelligence but as instruments for studying, evaluating, and refining intelligent systems themselves.

Key Elements of Perfect Prompts

Crafting an effective prompt is both a strategic and creative process—central to successful human-AI collaboration. Within the emerging field of prompt engineering, well-designed prompts function as clear instructions and structured frameworks. They enable artificial intelligence systems to interpret tasks precisely, produce relevant outputs, and maintain alignment with the user's intended goals and tone.

The quality of a prompt depends on a combination of linguistic, structural, and contextual features. A prompt must clearly communicate intent, define boundaries, and convey specific expectations. Whether the task involves analysis, writing, summarization, or dialogue, the following components are essential to ensure that AI responses are coherent, accurate, and professionally useful.

1. Specificity

Specificity ensures that the AI focuses precisely on the intended objective. Prompts that lack specificity often produce vague, generalized, or unfocused outputs, a limitation sometimes described as *hallucinated competence.* In professional contexts, specificity requires clearly defining the task, domain, constraints, and expected format of the output.

> ***Example Prompt***
> *"You are a market research analyst. Prepare a comparative report evaluating the customer satisfaction levels of three competing mobile banking apps in West Africa. Focus on usability, transaction speed, and customer support. Present findings in a structured table followed by a 200-word analytical summary."*

This prompt establishes a clear role, task, scope, performance criteria, geographic focus, and output format. By tightly defining these parameters, the model is prevented from generating abstract commentary or irrelevant generalizations. Specificity enables the AI to concentrate on targeted analysis, improving precision, relevance, and professional usability.

2. Clarity

Clarity emphasizes linguistic precision, logical structure, and unambiguous phrasing. Vague language, loosely defined instructions, and poorly sequenced requests increase the risk of misinterpretation and diluted output quality. Effective prompts rely on direct instructions, active verbs, and coherent sequencing.

Example Prompt

"Summarize the main causes of urban flooding in coastal West African cities. Then explain how improved drainage infrastructure and urban planning policies could reduce flood risk. Limit the response to 300 words."

This prompt structures the task in a clear analytical sequence: cause identification followed by solution analysis. By using direct instructions and defined output limits, it minimizes ambiguity and ensures that the response remains focused, logically organized, and contextually relevant.

3. Context

Context defines the situational, operational, or environmental conditions under which the AI must perform. Without adequate context, models often default to generic explanations that fail to address real-world complexities. Context enables the AI to tailor responses to specific scenarios, industries, audiences, or constraints.

> ***Example Prompt***
> *"You are assisting a nonprofit organization launching a digital literacy program for rural communities in Ghana. Design a training curriculum that addresses limited internet access, low smartphone penetration, and multilingual learning environments."*

By providing geographic, technological, social, and infrastructural context, this prompt anchors the model's reasoning within realistic constraints. The AI is guided to produce solutions that are practical, culturally sensitive, and operationally feasible rather than theoretically ideal but impractical.

4. Relevance (Negative Prompting)

Relevance ensures that AI outputs remain tightly aligned with the user's core objective. One effective strategy for enforcing relevance is *negative prompting,* which explicitly instructs the model on what to exclude. This technique prevents topic drift and analytical dilution.

> ***Example Prompt***
>
> *"Explain the principles of sustainable architecture for commercial office buildings. Exclude residential housing design, interior decoration, and landscaping. Focus only on energy efficiency, material sustainability, and climate-adaptive building systems."*

The exclusionary instruction enforces topical discipline, preventing the model from incorporating loosely related material. In complex domains where multiple concepts overlap, negative prompting sharpens analytical focus and significantly improves conceptual precision.

5. Conciseness

Conciseness ensures that prompts communicate sufficient direction without unnecessary elaboration. Overly verbose prompts introduce cognitive noise and may obscure core objectives. Effective prompts strike a balance between completeness and brevity.

> ***Example Prompt***
>
> *"Provide a 120-word executive summary outlining the business benefits of adopting cloud-based accounting software for small enterprises."*

The imposed length constraint compels the model to prioritize essential insights rather than peripheral explanations. Conciseness is especially valuable in executive communication, decision briefs, and professional reporting contexts where clarity and efficiency are critical.

6. Constraints

Constraints define mandatory boundaries governing tone, format, structure, length, or stylistic standards. They serve as quality-control mechanisms, ensuring outputs align with professional, institutional, or publication requirements.

Example Prompt

"Write a technical guide explaining blockchain technology for undergraduate computer science students. Use a formal academic tone, include headings and bullet points, and limit the document to 800 words."

By specifying tone, structure, formatting, and length, this prompt ensures the output meets pedagogical and academic standards. Constraints enable predictable, repeatable results, which is essential for educational materials, technical documentation, corporate communication, and scholarly publishing.

7. Consistency

Consistency ensures stylistic, logical, and structural uniformity across multiple AI-generated outputs. This is particularly important for large-scale projects such as training manuals, policy documents, branding campaigns, and multi-part publications.

> ***Example Prompt***
> *"Using the same structure, tone, and formatting style as the previously generated onboarding manual, produce a cybersecurity awareness guide for new employees."*

This instruction leverages the AI's contextual continuity to maintain coherent presentation across document sets. Consistency reduces editing time, strengthens professional credibility, and supports institutional branding and communication standards.

Conclusion

Crafting high-quality prompts is foundational to maximizing the value and reliability of AI systems. By incorporating these key elements—specificity, clarity, relevance, context, conciseness, and consistency—users can design prompts that deliver more accurate, meaningful, and task-appropriate responses.

In essence, perfect prompts are not only well-structured but also purposeful. They reflect the user's intent and guide the AI to act with clarity, creativity, and professional precision. As AI becomes increasingly embedded in our workflows, mastery of these principles will determine how effectively we communicate with, and through, intelligent systems.

Advanced Prompting Techniques

As AI language models continue to evolve in complexity and capability, so too must the ways in which professionals engage with them. While foundational prompt elements—such as clarity, specificity, and context—remain essential, more advanced strategies enable users to extract richer, more structured, and more accurate outputs from these models. These techniques are especially useful when addressing complex reasoning, ambiguous tasks, or iterative processes.

In this section, we examine five key prompting strategies: zero-shot prompting, few-shot prompting, chain-of-thought prompting, Iterative Prompting, and Prompt Chaining, Each method represents a distinct way to guide large language models based on the structure and amount of information included in the prompt.

1. Zero-Shot Prompting

Zero-shot prompting involves assigning a task without providing examples, templates, or stylistic guidance. The AI relies entirely on its pre-trained knowledge to generate a response.

This technique is best suited for situations requiring quick explanations of established concepts, high-level overviews, or introductory summaries where conventions are widely shared and the risk of misinterpretation is low.

> ***Example Prompt***
> *"Explain the concept of supply chain resilience and identify its core components in modern manufacturing."*

With no examples or reference outputs provided, the model relies entirely on its pre-trained knowledge to generate a response. This approach is efficient and fast, making it ideal for exploratory learning, brainstorming, or clarifying foundational ideas.

2. Few-Shot Prompting

Few-shot prompting improves precision by providing the model with a small number of representative examples that illustrate the desired structure, tone, or approach. Rather than explaining expectations abstractly, the user demonstrates them concretely.

Across disciplines, this mirrors how professionals learn from exemplars, whether lesson samples, reports, proposals, or design briefs.

> ***Example Prompt***
> *"I will provide two examples of executive summaries used in sustainability reports. Using these as structural and stylistic references, draft a similar executive summary for a mid-sized renewable energy company.*
>
> *Example 1:*
> *'This report outlines our environmental commitments, key performance indicators, and progress toward net-zero targets.'*
>
> *Example 2:*
> *'The following summary highlights strategic initiatives, measurable outcomes, and stakeholder impact.'*
>
> *Task: Draft the new executive summary."*

Few-shot prompting is particularly effective for enforcing consistency, aligning outputs with organizational standards, and reducing post-editing effort.

3. Chain-of-Thought Prompting

Chain-of-Thought prompting requires the AI to articulate its reasoning through a structured sequence of logical steps rather than producing a single, conclusory answer. This technique prioritizes transparency and analytical rigor.

It is especially valuable for tasks involving evaluation, comparison, decision-making, or problem diagnosis across disciplines.

> ***Example Prompt***
> *"Evaluate whether implementing a remote-first work model would be suitable for a mid-sized consulting firm. Do not provide a final recommendation immediately. Instead, explain your reasoning step by step"*

By requiring the model to "show its reasoning," Chain-of-Thought prompting exposes assumptions, logical gaps, or oversimplifications that might otherwise remain hidden. This makes it particularly useful for strategic planning, research analysis, and complex professional judgment.

4. Iterative Prompting

Iterative prompting treats AI interaction as a multi-stage process rather than a one-time instruction. The user progressively refines the output through feedback, clarification, and adjustment.

This approach reflects real-world professional workflows, where drafts evolve through review and revision rather than emerging fully formed.

> ***Example Prompt Sequence***
> *Turn 1: "Summarize the main challenges organizations face when adopting artificial intelligence."*
> *Turn 2: "Good. Now expand the summary to include ethical and workforce-related challenges."*
> *Turn 3: "Refine this into a concise briefing note suitable for senior management."*

Iterative prompting recognizes that quality improves through dialogue. By guiding refinement step by step, users maintain control over depth, tone, and relevance, while allowing the model to progressively sharpen its output.

5. Prompt Chaining

Prompt chaining links multiple prompts so that the output of one becomes the structured input for the next. Each step performs a distinct function within a larger workflow.

This technique is particularly effective for managing complex, multi-stage tasks that would overwhelm a single prompt.

> ***Example Prompt Chain***
> *Step 1: "Summarize the key findings from this customer feedback dataset."*
> *Step 2: "Using that summary, identify the three most critical improvement areas."*
> *Step 3: "For each identified area, propose actionable recommendations and success metrics."*

By decomposing complexity into discrete stages, prompt chaining improves focus, depth, and coherence at each step. It also allows users to intervene, adjust direction, or validate assumptions before proceeding further.

Table 1.2: *Summary Table of advanced prompting techniques and their unique function in professional practice*

Prompting Technique	Purpose	Professional Use Case	Key Advantages
Zero-Shot Prompting	Generate output using general knowledge	Definitions, overviews, ideation	Speed and efficiency
Few-Shot Prompting	Guide structure and style using examples	Reports, summaries, templates	Improves consistency and accuracy
Chain-of-Thought Prompting	Enforce step-by-step reasoning	Analysis, evaluation, decision-making	Makes logic transparent
Iterative Prompting	Refine outputs through feedback	Drafting, polishing, adaptation	Enables controlled improvement
Prompt Chaining	Sequence multi-stage tasks	Research workflows, strategy development	Manages complexity effectively

Conclusion

As summarized in Table 1.2, advanced prompting techniques allow professionals to move beyond surface-level interaction toward deliberate reasoning control. The ability to select and combine methods, such as using Few-Shot prompting for structured outputs and Chain-of-Thought prompting for analysis, enables users to shape both the depth and reliability of AI-generated content.

When applied strategically, these techniques transform Large Language Models from passive response generators into active cognitive collaborators. Mastery of advanced prompting is therefore not domain-specific expertise, but a transferable professional skill essential for effective work in an AI-augmented environment.

Assigning Roles for Effective Prompting

Role-based prompting, often described as persona engineering, is a powerful technique for improving the relevance, depth, and professional alignment of AI-generated outputs. It involves explicitly defining the role, expertise level, or perspective the AI should adopt before executing a task.

In professional settings, generic prompts often produce generic outputs that resemble surface-level explanations or introductory material. By assigning a role, the user signals the model to emulate the reasoning patterns, vocabulary, priorities, and decision-making posture associated with a specific professional identity. This framing helps the AI move beyond default generality and respond in ways that better reflect real-world expertise and expectations.

This section examines three foundational role-based prompting techniques applicable across disciplines: the Role (Identity) technique, the Act As (Behavioral) technique, and the Assume (Perspective) technique.

1. The "Role" Technique

The Role technique instructs the AI to adopt a defined professional identity before generating content. It establishes a stable persona and is most effective when the task requires domain expertise, seniority, or discipline-specific depth.

> ***Example Prompt***
>
> *"You are a senior sustainability consultant with fifteen years of experience advising multinational manufacturing firms. Prepare a strategic overview of how circular economy principles can be integrated into an existing global supply chain."*

By specifying both the professional role and level of experience, the prompt cues the model to avoid introductory explanations and to apply advanced terminology, industry awareness, and pragmatic judgment. Seniority indicators tend to produce outputs that are more strategic, risk-aware, and implementation-focused rather than purely theoretical.

The Role technique is especially effective for strategic planning, professional reports, policy drafting, instructional design, technical documentation, and executive-level analysis.

2. The "Act As" Technique

The Act As technique emphasizes behavior rather than identity. It instructs the AI to perform a task in the manner of a particular professional actor, focusing on approach, tone, and situational judgment.

This method is particularly useful for dynamic scenarios where strategy, communication style, or audience engagement matters as much as factual correctness.

> ***Example Prompt***
> *"Act as a product manager presenting a new software feature to non-technical stakeholders. Explain the feature's value proposition, address likely concerns, and maintain a confident but accessible tone."*

Here, the instruction guides the model's communicative behavior rather than its credentials. The model is encouraged to prioritize clarity, persuasion, and audience alignment. This allows users to rehearse presentations, refine messaging, and explore alternative delivery strategies in advance of real-world interactions.

The Act As technique is well suited to teaching simulations, leadership communication, sales strategy, public engagement, training scenarios, and cross-functional collaboration.

3. The "Assume" Technique

The Assume technique directs the AI to adopt a specific analytical or critical perspective. Rather than performing a task from a neutral stance, the model is instructed to evaluate content through a particular lens or hypothetical viewpoint.

This approach is especially valuable for stress-testing ideas, uncovering blind spots, and anticipating alternative interpretations.

> ***Example Prompt***
> *"Assume the perspective of a skeptical data privacy advocate. Review the following proposal for an AI-driven customer analytics platform and identify potential ethical, social, and transparency concerns."*

By assigning a defined perspective, the model departs from default balance and produces a more pointed, critical analysis. This enables users to refine arguments, strengthen proposals, and prepare responses to anticipated objections.

The Assume technique is particularly effective for peer review, risk assessment, ethical analysis, policy evaluation, and innovation testing across disciplines.

Conclusion

Assigning roles is one of the most effective ways to elevate AI-generated outputs from generic responses to context-aware, professionally aligned work products. Users should begin with the Role technique when expertise and depth are required, deploy Act As prompting for communicative or strategic tasks, and apply the Assume technique when evaluating ideas from alternative viewpoints.

When combined with advanced prompting methods such as chain-of-thought reasoning or prompt chaining, role-based prompting transforms artificial intelligence from a passive response generator into a disciplined, adaptable collaborator capable of supporting complex interdisciplinary workflows.

Common Prompting Mistakes

Prompt engineering plays a central role in enabling effective and productive interaction between humans and artificial intelligence systems. Well-constructed prompts guide models toward relevant, accurate, and contextually appropriate outputs. However, many users, including experienced professionals, make recurring mistakes that reduce output quality and reliability.

Common errors such as vague instructions, excessive complexity, hidden bias, missing context, or contradictory requirements can hinder an AI system's ability to interpret user intent. This chapter examines these frequent pitfalls and presents corrective strategies that improve clarity, precision, and outcome alignment across professional domains.

1. Vague or Ambiguous Prompts

One of the most common prompting mistakes is vagueness. Prompts that lack specificity force the AI to make assumptions, which can lead to inconsistent, generic, or irrelevant responses.

Vague Prompt

"Write a story about a person's day."

This prompt provides no details about setting, purpose, tone, or focus. As a result, the AI may generate an output that does not align with the user's expectations.

Improved Prompt

"Write a 300-word short story about a nurse working a night shift in a busy urban hospital, focusing on an unexpected challenge and how it is resolved."

The improved version defines length, profession, environment, and narrative focus. Clear parameters reduce ambiguity and produce more targeted results.

Key Principle: Precision reduces guesswork. The clearer the task, the more relevant the output.

2. Overly Complicated or Excessively Long Prompts

While context is important, prompts that contain too many instructions, goals, or conditions can overwhelm the model and dilute output quality.

Overly Complex Prompt

"Imagine you are a successful entrepreneur who has just launched a new technology startup. Your company has secured funding and now needs a comprehensive marketing strategy that includes target audience analysis, brand positioning, advertising channels, influencer partnerships, social media strategy, growth timelines, and performance metrics in a 10-page report."

This prompt combines numerous objectives and deliverables, increasing the risk of a scattered or shallow response.

Improved Prompt

"Develop a structured marketing strategy for a newly funded technology startup. Include target audience analysis, brand positioning, promotional channels, and key performance indicators."

The refined version maintains essential goals while removing unnecessary narrative framing and excessive length requirements.

Key Principle: Provide sufficient direction, but avoid cognitive overload. Focus improves coherence.

3. Biased or Leading Prompts

Prompts that contain assumptions, emotionally loaded language, or predetermined conclusions can steer AI systems toward one-sided or distorted outputs. Because language models are designed to follow the framing of the prompt, they may amplify the bias embedded in the instruction rather than provide balanced reasoning. This can be particularly problematic in professional, academic, or policy contexts where neutrality and analytical rigor are essential.

Biased Prompt

"Explain why remote work is more productive than office work."

This prompt presupposes a conclusion and encourages selective reasoning. The model is likely to emphasize supporting arguments while overlooking legitimate counterpoints, leading to an incomplete and potentially misleading analysis.

Improved Prompt

"Compare the advantages and disadvantages of remote work and office-based work in terms of productivity, collaboration, and employee well-being."

The revised prompt removes the assumption and introduces balanced evaluation criteria. This encourages the AI to explore multiple perspectives, resulting in a more comprehensive and credible response.

Key Principle: Prompts should invite analysis, not dictate conclusions. Neutral framing improves objectivity and informational value.

4. Lack of Contextual Information

AI systems rely heavily on contextual signals to determine scope, tone, and relevance. When prompts lack background details such as audience, purpose, professional role, or situational constraints, outputs tend to default to generic or overly broad responses that may not serve the user's needs.

Prompt Lacking Context

"Write a speech about climate change."

This instruction omits audience, purpose, and setting. As a result, the AI must guess the appropriate tone, depth, and focus, increasing the risk of a mismatched response.

Context-Rich Prompt

"You are an environmental science teacher addressing high school students. Write a five-minute speech

explaining why climate change mitigation matters and how young people can contribute to solutions."

By specifying the speaker's role, audience level, and objective, the revised prompt anchors the response in a clear communicative situation. This improves relevance, tone alignment, and practical usefulness.

Key Principle: Context transforms abstract tasks into purpose-driven communication.

5. Inconsistent or Contradictory Prompts

Prompts containing conflicting requirements create interpretive tension for the AI. When instructions cannot logically coexist, the model may produce blended, incoherent, or stylistically inconsistent outputs.

Contradictory Prompt

"Write a formal academic analysis of social media trends using casual slang and humor throughout."

The request combines incompatible stylistic expectations. *"Formal academic analysis"* implies scholarly tone and structure, while *"casual slang and humor"* suggests informality. The AI may struggle to reconcile these directions, leading to uneven or confusing results.

Consistent Prompt

"Write a formal academic analysis of social media trends, using clear language and evidence-based reasoning."

This version aligns tone, purpose, and expectations, enabling the AI to deliver a coherent and stylistically appropriate response.

Key Principle: Prompts must be internally consistent. Alignment between tone, purpose, and format ensures clarity and predictability.

6. Ignoring Tone or Style

Tone shapes how information is received. When prompts fail to specify tone, audience, or communication style, AI-generated outputs may feel mismatched, overly technical, too casual, or emotionally inappropriate for the context.

Unspecified Tone Prompt

"Write an article about workplace stress."

This lacks audience cues and emotional framing. The AI might produce a clinical report, a casual blog post, or a general essay, any of which could miss the user's intent.

Specified Tone Prompt

"Write a 700-word supportive and practical article for team managers on recognizing and reducing workplace stress among employees."

The revised prompt clarifies tone (supportive and practical), audience (team managers), and purpose (recognition and reduction). These cues guide vocabulary, examples, and structure.

Key Principle: Tone instructions align emotional register and communication style with audience expectations.

7. Asking for Impossible or Unsupported Information

AI systems generate responses based on patterns learned during training. They do not possess real-time awareness, predictive certainty, or access to private or future data. Prompts requesting unknowable, speculative, or unverifiable information increase the likelihood of fabricated or misleading outputs.

Unsupported Prompt

"List the top ten companies that will dominate the global market in 2035."

This task requires definitive knowledge about the future, which no model can reliably provide. The response may appear confident but would be speculative rather than evidence-based.

Supported Prompt

"Describe current technological and economic trends that analysts believe could influence which industries grow significantly over the next decade."

This alternative focuses on present knowledge and informed analysis rather than prediction. It allows the AI to provide meaningful insights grounded in observable patterns.

Key Principle: Ask for analysis of known information, not certainty about unknown outcomes. This reduces the risk of misleading or fabricated responses.

Conclusion

Prompt design is a deliberate and strategic practice. Mistakes such as vagueness, excessive complexity, bias, missing context, contradictions, tone neglect, and unrealistic requests reduce the usefulness and reliability of AI-generated outputs.

An effective prompt acts as both a map and a mission: it defines direction while clarifying purpose. By recognizing and correcting these common errors, professionals across disciplines can significantly improve the precision, relevance, and credibility of their interactions with artificial intelligence systems.

PART III

AI Tools and Their Effective Use Cases

As explored in earlier chapters, the quality of AI outputs depends not only on prompt design but also on understanding the platforms that receive those prompts. Each AI tool offers unique strengths, interaction modalities, and capabilities that can shape professional workflows. Learning to navigate and leverage these tools enables users to maximize impact, accelerate productivity, and apply prompt engineering in real-world settings.

This chapter introduces widely used AI systems that transform well-structured prompts into powerful professional outputs. From conversational assistants and multimodal generators to productivity enhancers and creative engines, these platforms support drafting, design, analysis, automation, and multimedia generation.

Professionals who master how these tools work will be better positioned to integrate AI into workflows across domains such as research, communication, design, analytics, and content creation.

ChatGPT

ChatGPT is a state-of-the-art conversational AI developed by OpenAI, widely used for text generation, reasoning, code writing, document analysis, and creative work. It operates via natural language prompts and supports multimodal inputs in advanced tiers.

Features and Capabilities

ChatGPT can conduct deep reasoning, summarize and analyze documents, generate and debug code, and support collaborative workflows. It also includes image generation (via DALL·E and related models) and, in advanced plans, video generation with OpenAI's **Sora 2** models, which produce short prompted video with synchronized audio and better physical realism than earlier video tools. Sora exemplifies the frontier of text-to-video creation, capable of generating short, narrative video clips with sound and scene continuity.

How to Access ChatGPT

ChatGPT is accessible at **chat.openai.com** and via mobile apps. The free tier offers basic capabilities with models such as GPT-4o. Paid options like ChatGPT Plus ($20 per month) provide priority access to more advanced models and tools such as Sora and file interpretation.

Gemini

Gemini is Google DeepMind's flagship multimodal AI model family. It supports text, image, audio, and extended reasoning tasks with deep contextual understanding and integration into Google services.

Features and Capabilities

Gemini enables multimodal interaction, document summarization, spreadsheet analysis, coding assistance, and deep contextual understanding. The Gemini models integrate smoothly with Gmail, Google Docs, Drive, Google Cloud, and Android, facilitating workflows such as collaborative editing, data interpretation, and research synthesis. Recent versions emphasize enhanced reasoning and multimodal output generation.

How to Access Gemini

Users can access Gemini via **gemini.google.com** or through integrated Google products. A free tier offers basic capabilities, and premium plans unlock advanced features such as extended memory, larger context handling, and enhanced multimodal generation.

Perplexity AI

Perplexity AI is an AI-driven conversational knowledge assistant that combines real-time web retrieval with large language model generation. It is optimized for research, fact-checked synthesis, and decision support.

Features and Capabilities

Perplexity leverages retrieval-augmented generation (RAG) to provide answers backed by citations, making it particularly useful for research, academic writing, and professional inquiry. Features include conversational queries, multi-model chat (e.g., models such as GPT-4.1, Claude 3, Mistral variants), voice input, document upload, file analysis, image generation, and collaborative workspaces.

How to Access Perplexity AI

Users can visit **perplexity.ai** and sign in with Google or Apple accounts. The free plan supports browsing and basic queries, while paid plans include advanced models, enhanced multimodal tools, assistant customization, and larger context reasoning.

Microsoft Copilot

Microsoft Copilot embeds generative AI directly into the Microsoft 365 ecosystem, transforming everyday productivity applications into intelligent collaborators. Rather than acting as a separate interface, Copilot integrates with familiar tools such as Word, Excel, PowerPoint, Outlook, and Teams, enabling users to interact with content using natural language prompts.

Features and Capabilities

Copilot supports natural language commands for drafting documents, generating meeting summaries, deriving insights from data, automating emails, and creating presentations. It includes Copilot Vision for interpreting images and screens, voice-driven interaction, and screenshot analysis. Copilot Labs offers experimental tools that expand memory, reasoning, and interactive workflows.

How to Access Microsoft Copilot

Copilot is accessed via **Microsoft 365** applications or **copilot.microsoft.com**. Basic features are included with Microsoft 365, while Copilot Pro and enterprise licensing unlock advanced AI features and deeper integration.

Suno

Suno is an advanced AI music generation platform that enables users to create full-length musical compositions — including instrumental arrangements, vocals, and stylistic elements — from natural language prompts. It is designed to make high-quality music creation accessible to professionals in marketing, advertising, film, gaming, podcasting, and creative industries who may not have formal musical training.

Features and Capabilities

Powered by advanced generative audio models, Suno can produce full-length tracks with expressive vocal realism and stylistic nuance. Its creative tools include stylistic editing, vocal and instrumental blending, remastering, and collaborative features that allow teams to refine soundscapes and musical storytelling.

How to Access Suno

Users can access Suno at **suno.com** and sign up using email or third-party authentication. A free tier provides basic generation capabilities and limited credits. Subscription plans, such as Pro, expand track length, unlock advanced editing tools, provide commercial usage rights, and support higher-quality audio output.

Midjourney

Midjourney is a generative AI platform built for visual creation. It transforms text prompts into high-resolution images, and recent updates support early-stage video and 3D visual exploration. Midjourney is extensively used by artists, designers, brand teams, and visual storytellers to conceptualize, prototype, and produce artistic imagery on demand.

Features and Capabilities

Midjourney uses prompt-based image generation to support artistic exploration, visual storytelling, and design ideation. Features include prompt-driven styles, *inpainting* (editing within images), *outpainting* (expanding beyond borders), and region-based variation tools. It also supports voice prompts and emerging video generation models that convert static concepts into dynamic scenes.

How to Access Midjourney

Midjourney can be accessed through its web interface at **midjourney.com** or via its official Discord server, where users interact with the model using prompt commands. Access is subscription-based, with tiered plans offering varying levels of usage, generation speed, resolution, and commercial rights. Typical subscription tiers range from affordable entry levels to higher-capacity plans for heavy use or enterprise workflows.

Canva AI / Magic Studio

Canva AI, integrated into the Canva Magic Studio ecosystem, is an AI-enhanced creative platform that empowers users to generate and edit visuals, text, documents, and short-form video content using natural language prompts. It is designed for professionals in marketing, education, design, communications, and operations who need to produce polished creative work with speed and consistency.

Features and Capabilities

Canva AI includes tools such as Magic Write (text generation), Magic Media (AI-generated visuals), Magic Sheets (chart and data tools), and layout suggestions. Users can perform background removal, generate animations, edit images, and collaborate in real time. Voice prompting, video editing, and design automation extend its utility across marketing, education, and content creation.

How to Access Canva AI

Canva AI is available through **canva.com** with a free account that includes access to core tools. Full access to Magic Studio features — including advanced AI visuals, voice generation, animation tools, high-resolution exports, and extended brand asset management — requires a Canva Pro subscription.

Leonardo AI

Leonardo AI is a powerful generative content platform focused on visual and motion creation, designed to support creators, designers, developers, and teams working in concept art, marketing, entertainment, architecture, and game development.

Features and Capabilities

Leonardo supports detailed prompt customization, real-time editing via an AI canvas, and sketch-to-art transformations. Its tools include 3D texture generation, animation-ready image-to-video conversion, and fine control over visual elements. Leonardo's Phoenix model and motion features enable dynamic content suitable for concept art, game assets, and architectural visualization.

How to Access Leonardo AI

Leonardo AI is available at **leonardo.ai** with a free access tier that provides daily generation tokens. Paid plans expand token limits, unlock commercial licensing, enable team collaboration features, and offer API integration for production-scale use. Subscription tiers range from entry-level plans for individual creators to enterprise packages tailored to cross-department design workflows.

Cuebric

Cuebric is an AI-powered virtual production and environment generation platform that dramatically accelerates the creation of cinematic spaces and visual scenes. Designed for filmmakers, visual effects specialists, production studios, and immersive experience creators, Cuebric uses generative techniques to produce editable, high-fidelity environments in a fraction of the usual time.

Features and Capabilities

Cuebric uses advanced rotoscoping, AI inpainting, and depth extraction to convert 2D inputs into layered 3D-like scenes. It produces photorealistic sets, supports real-time adjustments, and exports assets compatible with tools like Unreal Engine, dramatically accelerating pre-production workflows.

How to Access Cuebric

Professionals can register at **cuebric.com** and choose from subscription plans that vary by export resolution, depth segmentation capabilities, and integration options with third-party tools. Licensing options support individuals, small studios, and enterprise teams working on large-scale productions.

InVideo AI

InVideo AI is a web-based, prompt-driven video creation platform that enables users to transform ideas into fully produced videos with minimal technical expertise. It is designed for marketers, educators, entrepreneurs, content creators, and businesses that need fast, scalable video production for digital platforms.

Features and Capabilities

InVideo AI drafts scripts, selects media assets from large libraries, generates voiceovers, adds subtitles and transitions, and applies dynamic editing such as scene deletion or visual adjustment without manual timeline manipulation.

How to Access InVideo AI

Users can sign up at **invideo.io** through a web browser. The Free plan includes limited weekly AI video generation and watermarked exports. Paid plans, such as Plus and Max tiers, expand generation time, provide access to premium stock media, remove watermarks, increase storage, and unlock advanced features like voice cloning and higher export limits.

Conclusion

These tools exemplify the diversity of AI platforms available to professionals today. Understanding each tool's capabilities, input requirements, and integration options allows users to select the best system for a given task. Whether generating text, images, audio, video, or interactive workflows, effective use of AI tools, combined with strong prompt engineering, enables professionals to work faster, think more deeply, and deliver greater impact.

Navigating the AI Tool Interface

The effective use of artificial intelligence (AI) tools begins with a clear understanding of their user interfaces. While large language models (LLMs) and multimodal platforms vary in design and terminology, their core functionalities are often consistent across conversational, research, and creative environments. In this guide, the ChatGPT interface is used as a representative example to illustrate these foundational functions.

The following sections describe key interface features, grouping related functions into thematic clusters for clarity. Where numbered references are made, they correspond to elements in an illustrative diagram (Figure 1.1), offering a visual complement to this discussion.

Core Interface Functions

Starting a Conversation (1–7)

1. **New Chat** – allows users to clear the previous dialogue and begin a new topic, similar to opening a fresh document in a word processor.

2. **Search Chat** – Enables quick retrieval of past discussions using keywords, saving time when revisiting earlier insights.

3. **Library** – Functions as a personal archive of past conversations, supporting continuity and reference.

4. **Sora** – connects to a creative generative model designed to produce realistic and imaginative scenes from text instructions, expanding multimodal capabilities for visual and narrative output.

5. **GPTs** – provides access to specialized versions of the AI tailored for specific tasks or professional domains, delivering more focused and efficient assistance.

6. **Projects** – Organizes conversations and outputs into structured workspaces, ideal for professionals managing multiple clients, research streams, or creative deliverables.

7. **Chats** – Provides quick access to active or pinned conversations, supporting continuity in daily use.

Professional Application: For content creators, educators, and researchers, starting with a clear context helps ensure accuracy, while specialized models and organized workspaces streamline domain-specific tasks.

Managing Work and History (8-8e)

8. **Account** – serves as a central hub for user identity, subscription status, and profile settings.

    8a. Upgrade Plan – displays subscription options with advanced capabilities, such as extended context windows, priority access, or expanded multimodal features

    8b. Customize ChatGPT – enables personalization of the AI's behavior and response style, aligning the system with specific professional needs.

    8c. Settings – provides a control panel for adjusting preferences, managing privacy safeguards, and configuring accessibility features.

8d. Help — offers access to troubleshooting resources, support documentation, and platform guides.

8e. Log Out — Ends the session securely.

Professional Application: In regulated environments such as healthcare, law, or project management, the ability to organize, retrieve, and securely manage conversations supports compliance and operational efficiency.

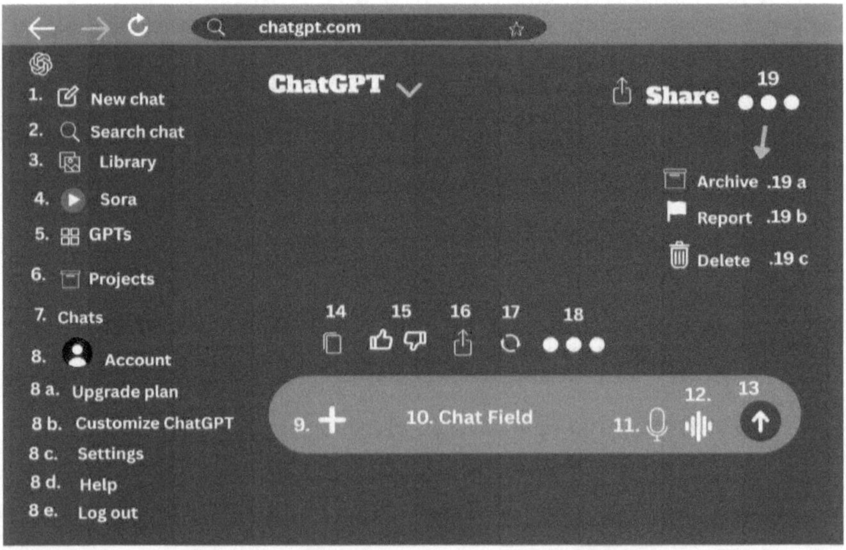

Figure 1.1: An Illustrative Diagram of the ChatGPT User Interface with numbered buttons and functions.

Input and Interaction (9–13)

9. **Upload Button** – Allows the addition of external files such as images or PDFs for analysis, summarization, or discussion.

10. **Chat Field** – is the primary input area for prompts, questions, or other text entries.

11. **Dictation Button** – converts spoken input into text within the chat field, especially useful for longer inputs or when typing is impractical.

12. **Voice Mode Button** – Activates spoken interaction with the model, offering a hands-free conversational experience.

13. **Submit Button** – Sends user input to the AI, prompting it to generate a response.

Professional Application: Multimodal input options enhance flexibility. Researchers may upload documents for summarization, while executives might use voice input to remain productive in fast-paced workflows.

Post-Interaction Functions (14–18)

14. **Copy Button** – duplicates the AI's response for easy transfer into external documents or reports.

15. **Thumbs Up / Thumbs Down Buttons** – provide direct feedback on response quality, where a thumbs up indicates a useful or accurate output, and a thumbs down signals issues or unsatisfactory results requiring refinement.

16. **Share Button** – Generates a link for collaboration or allows integration with productivity platforms and external tools.

17. **Try Again Button** – Prompts the AI to regenerate its most recent response, often yielding alternative phrasing, expanded detail, or different analytical perspectives.

18. More Button – Expands additional actions, including:

   18a. Branch in New Chat – Opens a new conversation thread beginning from the selected response, useful for exploring alternative directions without losing the original context.

18b. Read Aloud – Uses text-to-speech to present responses audibly, aiding accessibility and multitasking.

Professional Application: These functions support iterative refinement and collaborative workflows in consulting, research, and project delivery.

Conversation Management (19–19c)

19. **Header Menu (Three Dots)** – provides conversation-level controls, including:

19a. Archive – Moves conversations out of the active list into storage for later retrieval, preserving records without cluttering the workspace.

19b. Report – flags inappropriate, inaccurate, or problematic outputs for review and moderation.

19c. Delete – Permanently removes a conversation, an irreversible action that should be used with caution.

Professional Application: Effective use of these management tools supports data hygiene, ethical AI use, and compliance with organizational record-keeping policies.

Cross-Platform Equivalents

Although button labels and interface layouts differ across platforms, most LLMs and AI tools offer comparable functionalities. Recognizing these parallels supports seamless transitions between systems.

- **Content Generation and Specialization:** Tools such as ChatGPT's GPTs and Sora are analogous to Gemini's Storybook for narrative creation, Deep Research for analysis, and Canvas for visual brainstorming.

- **Visual Content Tools:** Gemini's Create Images mirrors image generation features in other AI platforms, including standalone visual tools.

- **Sharing and Exporting:** ChatGPT's sharing and export capabilities align with Gemini's unified Share menu, which includes options such as Export to Docs or Draft in Email. Perplexity AI, Microsoft Copilot, and other tools provide equivalent integrations.

- **User Feedback and Review:** The ability to report problematic content in ChatGPT corresponds with similar reporting tools in other platforms.

- **Accessibility and Interactivity:** Voice Mode, Dictation, and Read Aloud in ChatGPT map to comparable features such as Listen functions in other systems.

- **Content Verification:** Features that prompt verification against external sources, such as Gemini's Double-check response, are increasingly common across advanced platforms.

Professional Application: Understanding these similarities enables professionals to adopt new tools rapidly while preserving workflow continuity, accuracy, and efficiency.

Note on Specialized and Multimodal AI Tools

The principles discussed here apply beyond general-purpose LLMs. Specialized and multimodal platforms follow similar input–output logic:

- **Image generation tools** such as Midjourney, Leonardo AI, and Canva AI map user prompts to visual outputs.

- **Video and audio platforms** such as Cuebric AI, InVideo AI, and Suno employ prompt-based workflows to produce multimedia content.

Mastery of the fundamentals ensures smooth adoption of advanced platforms, empowering professionals to extend generative techniques across multiple media types.

Conclusion

The landscape of AI tools is evolving rapidly, yet the core principles of effective interaction remain constant. By mastering the foundational functions of an interface such as ChatGPT and recognizing comparable features in platforms like Gemini, Perplexity AI, and Microsoft Copilot, professionals can streamline workflows, improve collaboration, and enhance productivity.

Understanding an interface is not merely about learning buttons, it is about developing fluency in navigating AI systems. This fluency is essential for prompt engineering, where precision, efficiency, and adaptability directly influence outcomes. With this knowledge, you are equipped to engage confidently with the tools of today while remaining prepared for the innovations of tomorrow.

Integrating AI into Workflows

The previous chapter examined AI tool interfaces, highlighting how features such as file uploads, conversational branching, and output sharing form the operational foundation for effective human–AI interaction. While familiarity with these functions is essential, true value emerges when they are embedded within professional workflows to achieve measurable and repeatable outcomes.

Integrating AI into workflows positions prompt engineering as the bridge between human intention and machine capability. When prompts are designed strategically, repetitive tasks can be transformed into intelligent processes that improve speed, accuracy, creativity, and scalability.

This chapter outlines a structured approach to AI integration, identifies best practices for successful adoption, and presents interdisciplinary use cases. The goal is to move beyond knowing *how* to use AI tools toward embedding them as reliable collaborators in daily professional routines.

Key Steps for Integrating AI Tools

1. Audit the Workflow

Begin by identifying tasks that are repetitive, time-intensive, or knowledge-driven. These processes are ideal candidates for automation or AI-assisted augmentation. Examples include document drafting, data summarization, visual asset creation, report generation, and structured communication.

2. Define the Role of Prompts

Clarify the intended function of prompts within the workflow. Prompts may support ideation, automate content creation, enhance analytical reasoning, generate visuals or audio, or assist in decision preparation. Defining this role ensures alignment between human objectives and AI output.

3. Select the Appropriate AI Tool

Different tools excel in different modalities. For example, conversational models such as ChatGPT are well suited for drafting and analysis; research-oriented systems such as Gemini or Perplexity support information synthesis; visual tools such as Midjourney, Leonardo AI, or Canva AI enable image generation; and platforms such as InVideo

AI or Suno facilitate multimedia production. Selection should be based on task requirements, output format, and accessibility.

4. Create Modular Prompts
Complex tasks should be broken into structured stages. For instance, one prompt may generate an outline, another may refine tone or structure, and a third may summarize or adapt the content for a different audience. Modular prompting improves clarity, control, and output reliability.

5. Test, Refine, and Iterate
Pilot prompts on a small scale before full integration. Adjust wording, constraints, and context until results become consistent and aligned with professional standards.

6. Integrate with Existing Platforms
Embed AI outputs into established tools and systems. Microsoft Copilot can function within Word, Excel, and Teams, while outputs from ChatGPT or Perplexity can be transferred into presentation software, document platforms, or content management systems. Integration should enhance—not disrupt—existing workflows.

7. Monitor Output and Capture Feedback
Evaluate whether AI-generated results meet quality, accuracy, and compliance standards. Document effective

prompts and develop a shared prompt library to promote team-wide consistency and institutional learning.

Best Practices for Successful Integration

Effective AI integration requires structure, oversight, and strategic intent.

- **Start small and scale gradually.** Pilot AI in a limited workflow, such as summarizing meeting notes, before expanding into more complex processes like automated reporting systems.
- **Craft precise prompts.** Output quality is directly tied to prompt clarity, specificity, and contextual grounding.
- **Maintain ethical and professional standards.** Carefully review AI-generated content in sensitive domains such as healthcare, law, finance, or education. Transparency regarding AI assistance may be necessary in professional or academic contexts.
- **Keep humans in the loop.** AI should support, not replace, human expertise. Critical thinking, judgment, and final approval remain human responsibilities.
- **Document and share workflows.** Treat prompts as evolving organizational assets. A centralized

repository of effective prompts and prompt chains fosters consistency and long-term efficiency.

Professional Use Cases

Marketing and Communications

Content teams may use ChatGPT to generate article outlines and drafts, Midjourney or Leonardo AI to produce visual assets, and InVideo AI to convert written material into short promotional videos.

Education and Learning

Educators can employ conversational AI to design lesson plans or quizzes, Canva AI to produce instructional slides, and Suno to generate audio materials or creative learning aids.

Visual and Product Design

Design professionals can explore concept art or branding ideas using Midjourney or Leonardo AI, then refine layouts and presentation materials with Canva AI.

Corporate and Administrative Operations

Managers may rely on Microsoft Copilot to summarize emails, generate reports from spreadsheets, and draft meeting documentation, improving communication efficiency and decision readiness.

Media and Creative Production

Creators can combine Suno-generated music with visuals from Leonardo or Cuebric, assembling final productions through video platforms such as InVideo AI.

Conclusion

Integrating AI into workflows is not about replacing human expertise, but about amplifying creativity, efficiency, and analytical capacity through structured prompting. Whether drafting policies, developing campaigns, conducting research, or producing multimedia content, AI becomes a collaborative partner when guided by clear instructions and thoughtful workflow design.

Prompt engineering serves as the connective discipline between human intention and AI capability. Mastery of this skill enables professionals to transform everyday tasks into intelligent, scalable systems that enhance both productivity and innovation.

Evaluating and Selecting AI Tools

The rapid expansion of artificial intelligence platforms offers professionals unprecedented options for enhancing productivity, creativity, and decision making. Selecting the right AI tool requires more than considering popularity or brand recognition. It demands a thoughtful evaluation of each tool's capabilities, limitations, integration potential, and alignment with the specific needs of your workflow. This chapter outlines a structured approach to evaluating AI tools, helping you make informed decisions that maximize efficiency, reduce risk, and support prompt driven objectives.

Key Considerations for Selecting AI Tools

1. Define the Use Case

Begin by clearly identifying what you want the AI to accomplish. Some tools, such as ChatGPT, Perplexity, and Gemini, are particularly strong in text generation, summarization, explanation, and research support. Others, including Canva AI, Midjourney, and Leonardo AI, specialize in visual content creation. Platforms such as InVideo AI, Cuebric, and Suno focus on video and audio generation. Aligning a tool's primary function with your intended task ensures relevance, efficiency, and better output quality.

2. Evaluate Input and Output Modalities

Assess whether the tool accepts the input types you require, such as text, images, audio, or video, and whether it produces outputs in the formats, level of detail, and precision your workflow demands. For instance, if your goal is to create explainer videos directly from text prompts, a dedicated video generation platform such as InVideo AI may be most suitable. In contrast, if your workflow combines text and image generation, multimodal systems such as ChatGPT and Gemini can support both visual and textual outputs, offering greater flexibility for integrated tasks.

3. Assess Customization and Prompt Flexibility

Determine whether the tool supports prompt refinement, role assignment, structured instructions, and iterative interaction. Advanced versions of tools, such as ChatGPT Pro or Gemini Advanced, often support longer context windows and multimodal tasks, which allow greater control over tone, depth, structure, and continuity across interactions. This flexibility is especially important for professionals who rely on precise, repeatable outputs.

4. Review Accessibility and Platform Integration

Consider how and where the tool is accessed. Some platforms are entirely web based, while others are embedded within productivity ecosystems. For example, Microsoft Copilot is integrated into applications such as Word and Excel, which makes it particularly useful for professionals working within document heavy or data driven environments. Tools that function across desktop and mobile platforms can also provide added convenience for users who work in multiple settings.

5. Understand Pricing and Feature Tiers

Most AI tools provide free versions with limited capabilities and paid tiers that unlock advanced features. Evaluate pricing in relation to your expected usage volume, required output quality, and access to specialized functions such as high resolution image generation, voice synthesis, or advanced video editing. Subscription decisions should align with how frequently the tool will be used and how central it is to your professional workflow.

6. Examine Security and Compliance

When working with sensitive or proprietary information, carefully review each platform's privacy practices and data handling policies. Check whether the tool aligns with relevant data protection frameworks, such as the General Data Protection Regulation. Always read terms of service and avoid submitting confidential or regulated information unless the platform explicitly supports secure and compliant use.

The following tables, labeled 1.3a, 1.3b, and 1.3c, compare leading AI tools across three major categories, Conversational and Research Assistants, Creativity and Design Tools, and Productivity and Specialized Tools. Each table summarizes key features, input and output capabilities, pricing tiers, and typical professional use cases, providing a practical reference for tool selection.

Table 1.3a: Conversational and Research Assistants

Tool	Key Features & Capabilities	Input/ Output Types	Free Tier	Pro Features	Ideal Use Cases / Industries
ChatGPT	Multimodal input (Text, codes images),advanced reasoning, coding, file analysis	Text / Text, Code, image	Yes	Multimodal input, priority access, custom GPTs, internet browsing, advanced memory	Education, Software Development, Creative Writing, Business Communications
Gemini	Multimodal I/O, long-context memory, video & audio generation, Google Suite integration	Text, Image / Text	Yes	Long-context memory, multimodal tasks, coding support, real-time collaboration	Research, Productivity, Enterprise
Perplexity AI	Real-time search, citation-backed responses, document uploads, voice queries	Text image/ Text, Links	Yes	Document uploads, image generation, Labs, citation links	Research, Marketing, Decision Support

Table 1.3b: Creativity and Design Tools

Tools	Key Features & Capabilities	Input / Output Type	Free Tier	Pro Features	Ideal Use Cases / Industries
Midjourney	Fast generation of high-resolution images, style blending	Text/ image	No	High-resolution output, Draft Mode	Art, Design, Entertainment
Leonardo AI	Customizable models, sketch-to-art, 3D textures	Text / Image	Yes, limited	Fine-tuned image control, API access	Graphic Design, Games, Architecture
Canva AI	Text-to-image, presentation & video design, Magic Write, Magic Media, collaborative tools	Text / Image, Layouts	Yes	Brand kit sync, Magic Design, AI voice, collaboration tools	Marketing, Education, Social Media Content Creation

Table 1.3c: Productivity and Specialized Tools

Tool	Best For	Input / Output Types	Free Tier	Pro Features	Ideal Use Cases / Industries
Microsoft Copilot*	Embedded AI in MS Office apps (Word, Excel, PowerPoint, Teams), voice and image analysis	Text / Text, Charts	Yes*	Embedded in Office apps, advanced document & data tools	Enterprise workflows, Office productivity
Suno	Music generation with vocals, audio editing	Text / Audio	Yes	Extended track length, voice styling	Music production, Content Creation
Cuebric AI	Cinematic virtual production, 4K sets, Unreal Engine export	Text, Image / Video	Subscription only	Depth mapping, Unreal Engine export, VFX integration	Film, VFX, Virtual production
InVideo AI	Text-to-video, script drafting, voice cloning, subtitle addition	Text / Video	Yes	Voice cloning, HD export, script-based editing	Marketing, Education, Social media content creation

Note: *Available to Microsoft 365 users with Copilot access

Conclusion

Evaluating and selecting AI tools is a strategic process that requires aligning each platform's capabilities with your specific professional goals. By clearly defining use cases, assessing input and output modalities, comparing features, and considering integration, pricing, and security, professionals can build a reliable AI toolkit that enhances both productivity and creativity.

This structured approach, supported by comparative reference tables, helps readers navigate the complex AI landscape with greater confidence. Successful adoption of AI tools ultimately depends on balancing technological strengths with ethical awareness and human oversight, ensuring responsible, efficient, and sustainable outcomes.

Limitations of Artificial Intelligence

Artificial Intelligence offers powerful capabilities, but its adoption requires a clear understanding of inherent constraints. Despite the impressive outputs produced by tools such as ChatGPT, Gemini, Perplexity AI, and Midjourney, current AI systems exhibit technical, contextual, ethical, and operational limitations that may affect performance, reliability, and safety.

This chapter examines the most important limitations of contemporary AI systems, particularly large language models and generative platforms, and explains how professionals can reduce associated risks in prompt-driven workflows.

1. Lack of True Understanding

AI systems can generate language that appears coherent and contextually appropriate, but they do not possess genuine comprehension. These models operate by identifying statistical patterns in training data rather than understanding meaning in the human sense. As a result, they often struggle to sustain contextual coherence beyond the limits of a fixed context window, which varies by model and subscription tier. They may also misinterpret abstract, ironic, or culturally nuanced prompts that require deeper contextual awareness, and they can lose logical consistency over extended, multi-turn dialogues when topics become complex or shift unexpectedly.

Even advanced systems with extended context capabilities, such as premium versions of ChatGPT and Gemini, rely on pattern recognition rather than true cognitive understanding. To address this limitation, prompts should be written with explicit context, clearly defined objectives, and structured guidance that reduces the need for the system to infer unstated meaning.

2. Hallucinations and Misinformation

AI models can produce confident but incorrect or fabricated outputs, a phenomenon widely known as hallucination. This occurs when a model generates information that appears plausible but lacks factual grounding. It may misquote or invent references, provide inaccurate statistics, or offer fabricated legal, medical, or scientific claims.

This issue becomes particularly serious in fields that demand high precision, such as healthcare, law, finance, and journalism. Tools that incorporate live web information, such as Perplexity AI, can present citation-like material that appears credible but still requires verification. Likewise, conversational systems such as ChatGPT and Gemini may generate invented examples when prompted for factual data without strict evidentiary constraints.

To mitigate this risk, AI outputs should be treated as preliminary drafts or exploratory inputs, and all factual information should be verified using reliable, domain-specific sources before professional use or publication.

3. Prompt Sensitivity and Output Variability

AI systems are highly sensitive to the phrasing and structure of prompts. Small wording changes can produce noticeably different results, which presents challenges for workflows that require consistency. For instance, changing "Summarize the report" to "Can you provide a summary of this report" may influence tone or structure, while combining multiple instructions in a single prompt without clear organization can produce unfocused or inconsistent responses.

Even experienced prompt engineers encounter variability when prompts are not precisely structured. To reduce this inconsistency, professionals should use modular prompts, clear instruction hierarchies, and reusable prompt templates. Iterative refinement helps establish stable patterns that yield reliable outputs over time.

4. Bias and Ethical Risks

AI models can inherit and amplify biases embedded in their training data. These biases may relate to culture, gender, race, geography, or socioeconomic representation, and they can subtly influence outputs in ways that are problematic, particularly when prompts involve identity, ethics, or historical interpretation.

Such bias may appear in stereotypical language, skewed visual representations, or imbalanced framing in analytical outputs. To prevent the reinforcement of unintended bias, prompts should employ neutral and inclusive language, and outputs should be carefully reviewed before use in public, academic, or client-facing contexts. Cross-checking sensitive outputs with diverse perspectives or expert input further reduces the likelihood of biased outcomes.

5. Limited Depth of Domain Expertise

Although AI can simulate expert-like responses, it does not possess genuine professional specialization. Its performance is strongest in general tasks such as summarization, drafting, and brainstorming. Limitations become evident in areas that require deep technical or contextual knowledge, including complex legal analysis, advanced statistical modeling, or specialized scientific documentation.

Outputs such as computer code, financial projections, or technical explanations often appear convincing but may contain subtle inaccuracies. To address this limitation, AI-generated material in specialized domains should always be reviewed, validated, and refined by qualified professionals before implementation.

6. Security and Privacy Concerns

Many publicly accessible AI platforms operate through cloud-based systems that may store or analyze user inputs. Without clear enterprise-level safeguards, submitting confidential or regulated data can introduce privacy and compliance risks. This concern is especially relevant when working with health records, proprietary research, client data, or legally protected information.

To mitigate these risks, professionals should avoid entering sensitive information into public tools unless data protection terms are clearly understood. Using anonymized data, synthetic examples, or enterprise AI solutions with documented security and compliance measures can help ensure responsible and lawful use.

Conclusion

Understanding the limitations of contemporary AI systems is essential for responsible and effective use. While generative platforms and large language models provide powerful capabilities, they also present constraints related to comprehension, factual reliability, variability, bias, domain depth, and security.

By anticipating these limitations and designing prompts with clarity, context, and oversight, professionals can reduce risk and improve output quality. When paired with human judgment, ethical awareness, and domain expertise, AI becomes a valuable collaborative partner rather than an unquestioned authority.

AI Regulation and Compliance

As artificial intelligence becomes increasingly integrated into professional and institutional practices, understanding the legal and ethical frameworks governing its use is essential. Whether designing prompts for content creation, analysis, or multimedia production, regulatory awareness enables responsible application of AI technologies, mitigates legal and reputational risk, and supports ethical and compliant outcomes.

This chapter examines global regulatory trends as of January 2026, highlights jurisdiction-specific compliance requirements relevant to generative and large language models, and presents practical guidance for prompt engineers and professionals deploying AI responsibly.

Global Standards and Ethical Frameworks

International organizations have established ethical principles and standards that influence AI regulation and serve as shared benchmarks across sectors and jurisdictions.

The Organisation for Economic Co-operation and Development (OECD) Principles on Artificial Intelligence promote trustworthy AI rooted in transparency, accountability, fairness, human rights, and robust safety measures.[1]

The UNESCO Recommendation on the Ethics of Artificial Intelligence (2021) emphasizes inclusivity, human dignity, non-discrimination, and equitable access, advocating that AI systems protect fundamental freedoms and preserve human oversight.[2]

These global instruments are not legally binding, but they shape regulatory design and inform best practices internationally.

Jurisdictional Regulatory Frameworks

European Union

The European Union has enacted the Artificial Intelligence Act (AI Act), a comprehensive risk-based framework. While the Act became effective on 2 August 2024, the landscape is currently shifting due to the Digital Omnibus legislative package introduced in January 2026. This new proposal aims to simplify the compliance roadmap, potentially extending the deadline for high-risk systems (originally 2 August 2026) by 12 to 16 months to allow for the finalization of technical standards.[3]

The AI Act operates alongside the General Data Protection Regulation (GDPR), which continues to govern personal data processing.[4] Together, these form a governance regime impacting both EU operators and foreign AI providers serving EU users.

United States

The United States is currently navigating a period of federal and state regulatory friction. On 11 December 2025, a new federal Executive Order titled Ensuring a National Policy Framework for Artificial Intelligence was signed, proposing to preempt state AI laws deemed inconsistent with federal policy. To support this, the Department of Justice (DOJ) established an AI Litigation Task Force on 9 January 2026 to challenge specific state-level regulations.[5]

Despite federal moves toward preemption, California's Senate Bill 53 (SB 53), the Transparency in Frontier Artificial Intelligence Act, is currently in effect as of 1 January 2026. It requires developers of models trained with more than 10^{26} floating-point operations to publish transparency reports and implement whistleblower protections.[6]

Additionally, the California Consumer Privacy Act (CCPA) and the Children's Online Privacy Protection Act (COPPA) remain active, ensuring strict data protections for consumers and minors.[7] [9] Other states, such as Colorado, have laws scheduled for 2026 enforcement, though these face potential federal legal challenges.[8]

Canada

Canada's federal AI regulation remains in a state of transition. Bill C-27, which included the Artificial Intelligence and Data Act (AIDA), died on the Order Paper in January 2025 after the prorogation of Parliament. Currently, federal oversight is maintained through the Personal Information Protection and Electronic Documents Act (PIPEDA) and the Voluntary Code of Conduct on the Responsible Development and Management of Advanced Generative AI Systems.[10] [11]

United Kingdom

The United Kingdom maintains a principles-based approach led by existing regulators. AI systems must comply with the Data Protection Act 2018 and the UK GDPR. The Information Commissioner's Office (ICO) provides specific guidance on transparency and accountability in automated decision-making.[12]

Australia

Australia regulates AI through the Privacy Act 1988 and national AI ethics principles. Regulatory focus remains on ensuring fairness, accountability, and human-centered design through existing consumer and privacy protections.[13]

South Korea

South Korea has become a leader in APAC regulation with the AI Basic Act (Framework Act on the Development of Artificial Intelligence and Establishment of Trust), which officially took effect on 22 January 2026. The law mandates watermarking for AI-generated content, advance notification for generative AI users, and formal risk assessments for high-impact systems.[14]

Other countries, including Japan, Singapore, and China, are advancing national AI regulatory initiatives that address safety, accountability, and ethical use, contributing to a complex global regulatory environment.

Key Considerations for AI Implementation

- **Data Privacy and Protection:** Laws such as the GDPR, CCPA, and CPRA require transparent and lawful data handling. Prompt engineers should avoid including personally identifiable information in AI prompts without appropriate consent and safeguards.

- **Transparency and Explainability:** Many frameworks prioritize a right to explanation, where users should be able to understand how AI systems reach decisions. Documenting prompt design, workflow logic, and output validation supports these standards.

- **Fairness and Bias Mitigation:** Regulatory and ethical frameworks emphasize proactive bias assessment. Prompt design should use inclusive language and account for diverse user contexts to help mitigate biases in outputs.

- **Human Oversight and Accountability:** Across jurisdictions, human oversight remains a consistent requirement. Professionals should embed review stages in workflows to ensure AI-generated content is examined for accuracy, ethical soundness, and professional validity before external use.

Implementation Guidance for Prompt Engineers

Prompt engineers play a pivotal role in ethical and compliant AI deployment. Best practices include:

1. Using clear, neutral, and inclusive language in prompts.

2. Avoiding the inclusion of sensitive personal data when using public AI tools.

3. Maintaining version-controlled logs of prompt iterations, model responses, and verification steps.

4. Disclosing AI involvement where required in professional communication.

5. Aligning prompt frameworks with human-centred ethical principles and applicable laws.

These practices not only support legal compliance but also enhance trust, transparency, and professional integrity when using AI tools.

Future Trends in AI Regulation

AI regulation is rapidly evolving. Emerging trends may include:

- Mandatory labels and digital watermarking for all AI-generated multimedia.
- Public transparency registries for high-impact AI systems.
- Certification frameworks and standardized stress testing for frontier models.
- Algorithmic auditing focused on long-term societal impact.

Professionals should stay informed about these developments and update their workflows and prompt frameworks accordingly to maintain compliance and public trust.

Conclusion

AI regulation is advancing globally, with jurisdictions adopting diverse approaches that reflect local legal traditions and innovation priorities. Prompt engineers and professionals must integrate regulatory literacy into everyday practice, aligning prompt design with privacy, fairness, and transparency standards. Embedding compliance into AI workflows ensures that artificial intelligence remains trustworthy, equitable, and human-centered.

PART IV

Practical Prompt Packs for Professionals

Building on the foundations of AI concepts, the anatomy of effective prompts, and advanced methods such as zero-shot, few-shot, and chain-of-thought prompting, this chapter shifts from theory to direct professional application. It introduces structured, profession-specific prompt packs designed not just as reusable templates, but as guided learning tools that demonstrate how large language models can meaningfully support core workplace responsibilities.

Rather than presenting isolated prompt samples, this chapter encourages professionals to think critically about how prompts are constructed and adapted to real tasks. Through curated, real-world scenarios across multiple disciplines, readers learn to align AI capabilities with domain-specific challenges. The focus is on improving efficiency, strengthening analysis, enhancing communication, supporting documentation, and enabling more informed decision-making.

Effective professional use of AI does not depend solely on technical knowledge. It relies on judgment, clarity of intent, and the ability to evaluate and refine AI-generated outputs. Crafting precise, context-aware prompts, questioning assumptions, and iterating responsibly are what determine whether AI becomes a distraction or a true productivity partner. Prompting, therefore, is not just a technical technique, it is a cognitive discipline grounded in purpose and professional insight.

Using platforms such as ChatGPT, Gemini, Microsoft Copilot, Perplexity AI, and creative or multimodal tools like Suno, Midjourney, Cuebric, Leonardo, and InVideo, this chapter illustrates how AI can function as an intelligent collaborator. Each profession-focused section begins with a brief overview of the role, its common workplace challenges, and specific ways AI can provide support. This is followed by contextualized prompt scenarios that demonstrate not only what to ask, but how to ask effectively, reinforcing prompt design principles that are transferable across tools and industries.

Ultimately, these prompt packs serve two key purposes. First, they reveal the often-overlooked potential of AI to augment both routine and strategic professional work. Second, they equip readers with the practical prompting skills needed to use AI tools confidently, responsibly, and with measurable impact in their own fields.

Accountant

The Essential Role of an Accountant

Accountants are vital in maintaining the financial integrity of individuals, businesses, and institutions. They prepare accurate reports, ensure regulatory compliance, manage audits, and provide strategic financial insights to guide decision-making.

Common Challenges Faced by Accountants

Accountants often face demanding reporting deadlines, the need to interpret evolving tax regulations, and the challenge of identifying inconsistencies in large financial datasets. Communicating technical findings to non-specialists and adapting to frequent changes in accounting standards also add complexity.

How AI Simplifies Accounting Tasks

AI tools, especially large language models (LLMs), streamline accounting tasks by generating summaries, analyzing regulations, detecting data anomalies, and drafting professional correspondence. These models enhance clarity, and increase efficiency across diverse financial operations.

Crafting Effective Prompts for Accounting Tasks

This section presents practical, role-specific prompts to help accountants and financial professionals leverage large language models (LLMs) like ChatGPT, Gemini, and Microsoft Copilot in their daily work. These examples are grounded in real-world accounting challenges, from drafting financial reports and forecasting cash flow to automating tax research and fraud detection analysis.

1. Financial Report Drafting

Scenario

An accountant needs to prepare a narrative summary for a quarterly financial report to present to the executive board.

> **Prompt**
> *"You are a corporate financial reporter. Based on the attached financial data and key findings, draft a concise quarterly financial report. Include a clear executive summary highlighting the company's performance, a summary of key trends and KPIs, and a brief section on strategic insights for the next quarter."*

How It Works

Using a tool like Gemini or ChatGPT, first, enter the prompt. Next, upload the raw financial data in .csv or .xlsx, format, followed by a document containing your key findings from a .txt or .docx file. Then, submit. The AI will synthesize the information into a professional, narrative-driven report, saving significant time in the drafting process.

2. Tax Code Research

Scenario

An accountant needs to quickly research a specific section of the tax code to determine how it applies to a client's unique financial situation.

Prompt

"You are a tax specialist. Based on the provided tax code excerpt and client scenario, explain the tax implications for [specify client type, e.g., a self-employed freelancer]. Simplify the explanation using plain, non-legal language and cite the relevant section of the code."

How It Works

Using a tool like ChatGPT, Perplexity AI, or Gemini, first, enter the prompt. Next, specify the client in the prompt entry, and paste the tax code excerpt and a brief description of the client's situation from a text-based file (.txt, .docx) directly below it, and submit. The AI will provide a simplified, well-researched answer.

3. Cash Flow Forecasting

Scenario

An accountant needs to create a three-month cash flow forecast for a small business to ensure it has enough liquidity to cover upcoming expenses.

> **Prompt**
>
> *"You are a financial analyst. Based on the historical data and upcoming expenses provided below, generate a three-month cash flow forecast for a [specify business type]. Include inflows, outflows, and projected ending balances for each month. Identify any potential shortfalls."*

How It Works

Using a tool like ChatGPT or Microsoft Copilot, first enter the prompt. Next, specify business type in the prompt entry, and paste the historical financial data and a list of upcoming expenses from a text-based file (.txt, .csv) directly below it, and submit. The AI will generate a detailed forecast to guide financial planning.

4. Fraud Detection Analysis Support

Scenario

An accountant is investigating irregularities in monthly transaction logs for potential fraud indicators.

Prompt

"You are a forensic accounting assistant. Based on the attached transaction data, identify unusual patterns and potential red flags for fraudulent activity. Analyze for anomalous transactions, duplicate payments, and unauthorized vendors. Draft a preliminary potential fraud report highlighting these findings."

How It Works

Using a tool like Gemini or ChatGPT, first, enter the prompt. Next, upload the transaction data in a format like .csv or .xlsx. Then, submit. The AI will act as an investigative partner, helping you find a "needle in a haystack" and accelerating the preliminary analysis.

5. Journal Entry Generation

Scenario

An accountant needs to generate a series of complex journal entries for transactions that are tedious to create manually.

> **Prompt**
>
> *"You are a bookkeeper. For the transaction descriptions provided below, generate the corresponding journal entries. Include the date, account names, debit and credit amounts, and a brief description for each entry."*

How It Works

Using a tool like ChatGPT or Microsoft Copilot, first enter the prompt. Next, paste the list of transactions from a text-based file (.txt, .docx) directly below it, and submit. The AI will generate accurate, well-formatted journal entries, saving time and reducing manual errors.

6. Expense Analysis with Visual Output

Scenario

An accountant needs to analyze a company's expenses for the last quarter to identify spending trends, pinpoint major cost drivers, and find opportunities for cost reduction. They require a visual output for management.

Prompt

"You are a financial analyst. Based on the expense data provided, perform an expense analysis for the last quarter. Categorize expenses, identify the top five spending areas, and highlight any unusual trends. Create a bar chart to visually represent the expense breakdown."

How It Works

Using a tool like Gemini or ChatGPT, first, enter the prompt. Next, upload the expense data in a format like .csv or .xlsx. Then, submit. The AI will analyze the data and generate both a written report and a visual chart for clear, actionable insights.

Actuaries

The Essential Role of an Actuary

Actuaries analyze complex data to assess financial risk, design insurance products, and advise on pension plans, ensuring organizations make sound, data-driven decisions. By applying advanced statistical models, they help balance profitability with long-term financial stability.

Common Challenges Faced by Actuaries

Actuaries struggle with gathering high-quality data, updating assumptions to reflect changing markets, clearly communicating findings to non-technical stakeholders, and performing timely, detailed analyses under regulatory pressures.

How AI Simplifies Actuarial Tasks

AI assists actuaries by automating data cleaning, running simulations, and generating reports with intuitive explanations. Large language models can also help actuaries translate technical analyses into clear, stakeholder-friendly insights, improving efficiency and decision-making.

Crafting Effective Prompts for Actuarial Tasks

This section presents practical, role-specific prompts to help actuaries and risk professionals leverage large language models (LLMs) like ChatGPT, Gemini, and Perplexity AI in their daily work. These examples are grounded in real-world actuarial challenges, from analyzing mortality data and pricing new products to forecasting financial liabilities and communicating complex risk scenarios.

1. Mortality Rate Analysis

Scenario

A life insurance actuary needs to analyze historical mortality data to forecast future trends and update their pricing models.

Prompt

"You are a life insurance actuary. Based on the attached mortality data, analyze and identify key trends by age group, gender, and geographic region. Provide a mortality trend forecast for the next five years, including a brief summary of the key drivers and assumptions for the forecast."

How It Works

Using a tool like ChatGPT, Perplexity AI, or Gemini, first, enter the prompt. Next, upload the mortality data in a format like .csv or .xlsx. Then, submit. The AI will provide a data-driven analysis to inform your risk models.

2. Pricing a New Insurance Product

Scenario

An actuary is tasked with developing a pricing strategy for a new insurance product and needs to analyze market data, risk factors, and competitive pricing.

Prompt

You are a product pricing actuary. Based on the risk data and the attached competitive analysis, draft a preliminary pricing strategy for a new [product type, e.g., pet insurance]. Recommend a premium structure, justify the pricing assumptions, and highlight the key risk factors that could impact profitability."

How It Works

Using a tool like ChatGPT or Gemini, first, enter the prompt specifying the product type within the prompt entry. Next, upload the risk data, market analysis, and product details in a .csv, .xlsx, or .docx file. Then, submit. The AI will generate a structured pricing strategy to guide the development process.

3. Solvency and Capital Adequacy Report

Scenario

An actuary needs to draft a formal report on a company's financial health, demonstrating its ability to meet future obligations and maintain adequate capital.

> **Prompt**
>
> *"Assume the role of a risk management actuary. Draft a solvency and capital adequacy report for [insert company name] based on the attached financial data. The report should include an executive summary, an analysis of the key risks affecting solvency, and a conclusion on the company's ability to meet its future liabilities."*

How It Works

Using a tool like ChatGPT or Gemini, first, enter the prompt along with the company name within the prompt entry. Next, upload the relevant financial data in a format like .csv or .xlsx. Then, submit. The AI will generate a formal report, saving you time in drafting and structuring the document.

4. Reserve Calculation for Claims

Scenario

An actuary needs to quickly calculate the financial reserves required to cover future claims for a specific portfolio of policies.

Prompt

"You are a property and casualty actuary. Based on the claims data attached, calculate the actuarial reserves required for the portfolio. Use the [specify method, e.g., Chain Ladder Method] and provide a detailed breakdown of the calculations, assumptions, and a final reserve estimate."

How It Works

Using a tool like Gemini or ChatGPT, first, enter the prompt, ensuring you specify the actuarial method you want to use (e.g., Chain Ladder Method, Bornhuetter-Ferguson Method). Next, attach the claims data file in a structured format such as .csv or .xlsx. Then, submit. The AI will perform the complex calculations based on the specified method and provide a transparent, step-by-step breakdown of the reserve estimate.

5. Stress Testing Report with Visuals

Scenario

An actuary needs to prepare a professional report summarizing extreme stress scenarios for a pension fund's portfolio.

Prompt

"Act as an actuarial risk consultant. Using the attached Excel file containing portfolio data and stress test assumptions, draft a detailed report analyzing the impacts of a 40% market drop, a 200-basis-point interest rate hike, and a pandemic-level mortality spike. Include comparative charts illustrating solvency impacts."

How It Works

Using a tool like Gemini or ChatGPT, first, enter the prompt. Next, attach the Excel file containing the portfolio data and stress test assumptions. Then, submit. The AI will analyze the data, draft a professional report, and automatically generate the comparative charts you requested, providing a clear and comprehensive summary of the pension fund's financial health under extreme scenarios.

6. Interactive Dashboard Specification Brief

Scenario

An actuary needs to guide a development team in creating a dynamic Power BI dashboard for claims reserving analysis.

> **Prompt**
>
> *"Assume the role of a senior actuary. Using the attached dataset of historical claims, draft a specification brief for an interactive Power BI dashboard, detailing key metrics, recommended charts (e.g., trend lines, bar charts), filters, and layout guidelines."*

How It Works

Using a tool like ChatGPT, Gemini, or Microsoft Copilot, first upload the claims dataset. Next, enter the prompt and submit. The AI will produce a professional, developer-ready brief specifying key metrics, recommended visuals, and clear design elements, ensuring the dashboard meets both actuarial and user requirements without the need for manual transcription.

Agriculturist

The Essential Role of an Agriculturist

Agriculturists apply science and technology to improve crop productivity, manage soil health, and promote sustainable farming. Their expertise supports food systems, market forecasting, and agricultural innovation.

Common Challenges Faced by Agriculturists

Agriculturists frequently deal with unpredictable climate patterns, pest outbreaks, and the need to synthesize vast agronomic data. Communicating findings clearly to farmers, policymakers, or investors under time pressure adds further complexity.

How AI Simplifies Agricultural Tasks

AI tools help agriculturists analyze satellite imagery, forecast yields, and generate insights from environmental and financial data. Large Language Models automate reporting, summarize research, and assist in drafting extension materials—saving time while improving clarity and precision in agricultural decision-making.

Crafting Effective Prompts for Agricultural Tasks

This section provides practical, role-specific prompts to help agriculturists and farm managers leverage large language models (LLMs) like ChatGPT, Gemini, and Perplexity AI in their daily operations. The examples are grounded in real-world agricultural challenges, from data-driven crop planning and disease identification to livestock feed rationing, breeding programs, and poultry biosecurity plans.

1. Crop Rotation Planning

Scenario

An agriculturist needs a multi-year crop rotation plan to improve soil health, increase yields, and naturally manage pests and diseases.

> ***Prompt***
>
> *"You are a crop management specialist. Develop a three-year crop rotation plan for a farm in [region, e.g., West Africa]. Include a mix of cash crops, cover crops, and legumes, and provide a rationale for your selections."*

How It Works

Using a tool like ChatGPT, Perplexity AI, or Gemini, first enter the prompt. Next, specify the region within the prompt entry, and submit. The AI will generate a strategic multi-year plan with a clear rationale for each crop choice.

2. Pest and Disease Identification

Scenario

An agriculturist discovers signs of a pest or disease on a crop and needs a rapid, visual-based diagnosis to begin treatment.

Prompt

"You are a plant pathologist. Analyze the crop damage in the attached image and provide a differential diagnosis. Suggest initial control measures based on the symptoms and recommend further steps."

How It Works

Using a tool like ChatGPT or Gemini, first enter the prompt. Next, upload the image in a format like .jpeg or .png. Then, submit. The AI will analyze the visual evidence, offering potential diagnoses and guiding the user toward an effective solution.

3. Fertilizer Recommendation from Soil Tests

Scenario

An agriculturist has received soil test results and needs a tailored fertilizer recommendation to address nutrient deficiencies and optimize crop yield.

Prompt

"You are an agronomist. Based on the soil test results provided below, recommend a fertilizer application plan for [insert crop name]. Specify nutrient quantities (N-P-K), timing, and application methods. Justify your recommendations based on the data."

How It Works

Using a tool like ChatGPT, Perplexity AI, Microsoft Copilot, or Gemini, first enter the prompt, specifying the crop name in the prompt entry. Next, paste the soil test data from a text-based file (.txt, .docx) directly below it, and submit. The AI will provide a precise, data-driven fertilizer plan.

4. Drafting a Farm Management Plan

Scenario

A farmer is developing a formal business plan to secure a loan and needs to draft a comprehensive section on farm operations and resource management.

Prompt

"You are a farm business consultant. Draft a comprehensive farm management plan for a [specify farm type, e.g., 50-acre mixed vegetable farm]. Include sections on crop planning, labor management, equipment needs, and financial projections. Use a professional tone suitable for a business proposal."

How It Works

Using a tool like ChatGPT, Perplexity AI, or Gemini, first enter the prompt, specifying the farm type in the prompt entry. Next, submit. The AI will generate a professional and detailed farm management plan that can be used as a foundation for a business proposal or internal planning.

5. Breeding Program Planning

Scenario

An agriculturist wants to improve the genetic traits of their livestock herd. They need a long-term breeding program plan to achieve specific goals like disease resistance or increased productivity.

Prompt

"You are a livestock genetics consultant. Develop a three-year breeding program plan for a [specify livestock type, e.g., goat farm]. The goal is to improve [specify trait, e.g., milk yield or meat quality]. Include mating strategies, culling criteria, and key metrics for progress tracking."

How It Works

Using a tool like ChatGPT, Perplexity AI, or Gemini, first enter the prompt, specifying the livestock type and trait in the prompt entry. Next, submit. The AI will generate a long-term strategic plan outlining a detailed approach to improving the genetic quality of the herd over time.

6. Poultry Biosecurity and Disease Management Plan

Scenario

An agriculturist wants to create a comprehensive biosecurity plan to prevent the outbreak of common diseases in their poultry flock and manage a response if one occurs.

Prompt

"You are a poultry health specialist. Develop a detailed biosecurity and disease prevention plan for a [insert farm type, e.g., free-range chicken farm]. Include protocols for daily flock health monitoring, visitor and equipment control, sanitation schedules, and a clear emergency response plan for a suspected disease outbreak."

How It Works

Using a tool like ChatGPT, Perplexity AI, or Gemini, first enter the prompt, specifying the farm type in the prompt entry. Next, submit. The AI will generate a comprehensive biosecurity plan that outlines preventive measures and a step-by-step response strategy to protect your flock's health.

Architect

The Essential Role of an Architect

Architects design the built environment—residential, commercial, and civic spaces—by balancing functionality, aesthetics, safety, and sustainability. Their work shapes how people live and interact with their surroundings, making quality and precision fundamental to their profession.

Common Challenges Faced by Architects

Architects often struggle with iterative design revisions, managing client expectations, time-consuming documentation, and translating abstract ideas into visual concepts. Regulatory compliance and material specifications also add layers of complexity.

How AI Simplifies Architectural Tasks

AI—particularly large language models, can support architects by automating technical documentation, generating concept narratives, translating client briefs into spatial plans, and streamlining compliance research. It also enhances creative brainstorming through prompt-based design ideation and visual references.

Crafting Effective Prompts for Architectural Tasks

This section presents practical, role-specific prompts to help architects and designers leverage large language models (LLMs) like ChatGPT, Gemini, Perplexity, and multimodal tools like Midjourney and Leonardo AI in their daily work. These examples are grounded in real-world architectural challenges, from conceptual design and building code analysis to sustainable material selection and client communication.

1. Schematic Design Generation

Scenario

An architect needs to quickly generate several conceptual design ideas for a residential project based on a client's brief, exploring different layouts and aesthetic approaches.

> **Prompt**
>
> *"You are a design architect. Based on the client brief provided below, generate three distinct schematic design concepts for a residential home. Include a brief description of the layout, material palette, and the overall aesthetic for each concept."*

How It Works

Using a tool like ChatGPT, Perplexity AI, or Gemini, first enter the prompt. Next, paste the client brief and project requirements from a text-based file (.txt, .docx) directly below it, and submit. The AI will provide creative starting points to explore various design possibilities.

2. Sustainable Material Selection

Scenario

An architect is designing an eco-friendly building and needs to select sustainable materials that meet specific project goals for a particular region.

Prompt

"You are a sustainability consultant. Based on the project requirements and regional context provided below, recommend three sustainable material options for the building envelope. For each option, include its environmental benefits, cost implications, and local availability."

How It Works

Using a tool like ChatGPT or Gemini, first enter the prompt. Next, paste the project requirements (e.g., building type, climate, budget) from a text-based file (.txt, .docx) directly below it, and submit. The AI will offer data-informed material recommendations to support your sustainable design goals.

3. Building Code and Zoning Analysis

Scenario

An architect needs to analyze a project brief against local building codes and zoning ordinances to identify potential compliance issues early in the design phase.

> **Prompt**
>
> *"You are a code compliance specialist. Based on the building brief and zoning ordinance provided, identify any potential code and zoning issues for a [project type, e.g., multi-family residential building]. Highlight key sections of the code that require special attention."*

How It Works

Using a tool like Gemini or ChatGPT, first enter the prompt specifying the project type in the prompt entry. Next, upload the project brief and relevant zoning ordinance document in a .pdf or .docx file. Then, submit. The AI will cross-reference the documents to provide a preliminary compliance report, saving significant research time.

4. Sunlight and Shading Analysis

Scenario

An architect needs to perform a preliminary analysis of sunlight exposure and shading for a building design to optimize natural light and passive cooling.

Prompt

"You are a passive design analyst. Based on the geographical data and building orientation provided below, generate a report on sunlight exposure and shading for the building's façade throughout the day. Include visualizations of shadow patterns at key times (e.g., 9 AM, 12 PM, 3 PM) for both summer and winter."

How It Works

Using a tool like Gemini or Perplexity AI, first enter the prompt. Next, paste the location, building orientation, and design details from a text-based file (.txt, .docx) directly below it, and submit. The AI will analyze the data to provide an informed report and visual output.

5. Construction Cost Estimation (Conceptual)

Scenario

An architect needs a quick, conceptual cost estimate for an early-stage project to help the client understand the potential budget before committing to a detailed design.

Prompt

"You are a construction cost estimator. Based on the project description provided below, generate a preliminary cost estimate. Include a breakdown by major building systems (e.g., structure, envelope, MEP) and provide a total estimated cost with a rationale for key cost drivers."

How It Works

Using a tool like ChatGPT or Gemini, first enter the prompt. Next, paste the project description from a text-based file (.txt, .docx) directly below it, and submit. The AI will provide a high-level cost estimate to guide your early-stage project discussions.

6. Creating 3D Architectural Visualizations from 2D Drawings

Scenario

An architect needs to quickly create a compelling 3D visualization of a project for a client presentation without the time and cost of a full rendering. They want to transform a 2D drawing into a realistic, immersive environment.

Prompt

"Generate a photorealistic 3D architectural visualization for the attached 2D building plan. Place the building in a [location/setting, e.g., a naturalistic, sunlit urban park] and create a scene suitable for a client pitch."

How It Works

Using a specialized tool like Midjourney or Leonardo AI, first enter the prompt specifying the setting in the prompt entry. Next, upload the 2D architectural drawing in a format like .jpeg or .png. Then, submit. The AI will transform your 2D design into an immersive 3D scene, providing a powerful and efficient way to visualize your project.

Author

Essential Role of an Author

Authors craft compelling stories, nonfiction works, scripts, and other written content to inform, entertain, or persuade audiences. They plan narratives, develop characters, conduct research, and refine language to convey ideas clearly and engagingly.

Common Challenges Faced by Authors

Authors often struggle with writer's block, maintaining consistency across drafts, structuring complex narratives, editing large manuscripts, and conducting timely research to support plots or arguments—all while meeting tight deadlines.

How AI Simplifies Authoring Tasks

AI tools like ChatGPT, Gemini, and Perplexity AI assist authors with brainstorming plots, generating character descriptions, summarizing research, rewriting drafts for clarity or tone, and automating formatting. These tools help authors accelerate their creative process, maintain stylistic consistency, and reduce time spent on repetitive writing tasks.

Crafting Effective Prompts for Authoring Tasks

This section offers hands-on prompts showing how authors can leverage AI tools like ChatGPT, Gemini, and Perplexity AI to overcome creative blocks, polish manuscripts, and accelerate the writing process. Each example features a realistic scenario, an optimized prompt, and a clear explanation of how the AI-generated output supports professional-quality writing.

1. Breaking Writer's Block with Plot Ideas

Scenario

An author struggles to continue a mystery novel set in Victorian London and needs fresh twists.

> **Prompt**
>
> *"Act as a professional novelist and generate five original plot twists to revive a Victorian-era murder mystery, considering themes of betrayal, hidden identities, and societal scandal."*

How It Works

Using a tool like ChatGPT or Gemini, enter the prompt. Next, submit. The AI will deliver unique plot twists that spark creativity and help the author regain momentum, making progress on the stalled manuscript easier.

2. Drafting Compelling Character Backstories

Scenario

An author developing a historical romance needs vivid backstories for two protagonists to enrich emotional depth.

Prompt

"You are a historical fiction author. Create detailed backstories (250 words each) for two protagonists in an 1850s coastal village: a widowed schoolteacher and a reclusive lighthouse keeper, including formative events, motivations, and internal conflicts that drive their choices."

How It Works

Using a tool like ChatGPT or Gemini, first enter the prompt. Next, submit. The AI will produce rich, historically grounded character histories, helping authors establish authentic personalities and believable motivations. This depth enhances narrative cohesion and creates compelling arcs that keep readers engaged.

3. Enhancing Dialogue for Realism

Scenario

An author writing a contemporary thriller struggles to make tense conversations between a detective and suspect sound authentic.

Prompt

"You are a crime novelist. Rewrite the provided dialogue below to reflect a high-stakes interrogation between a seasoned detective and an evasive suspect. Maintain tension, realistic pacing, and psychological complexity."

How It Works

Using a tool like ChatGPT or Gemini, first enter the prompt. Next, paste your dialogue excerpt directly below it and submit. The AI will rework it with sharp, lifelike exchanges, ensuring characters speak naturally and interactions convey escalating stakes. This helps authors produce immersive scenes that grip readers and advance plots convincingly.

4. Professional Review for a Fiction Novel

Scenario

A novelist seeks an in-depth review of their completed fiction manuscript to evaluate character development, plot cohesion, and genre engagement.

Prompt

"You are a professional book reviewer. Read the attached fiction manuscript and craft a 1,000-word critical review discussing plot structure, pacing, character arcs, dialogue authenticity, and genre fit. Maintain a balanced, constructive perspective, identifying both strengths and areas for improvement."

How It Works

Using a tool like ChatGPT, Perplexity AI, or Gemini, first upload the manuscript in Word or PDF format. Next, enter the prompt and submit. The AI will provide a thorough, professional review, equipping authors with actionable insights to enhance storytelling quality and save the time and cost of a human critique.

5. Summarizing Research for Nonfiction Writing

Scenario

An author drafting a nonfiction book on climate change needs to condense a 40-page IPCC report into a digestible summary for a chapter.

Prompt

You are a nonfiction author. Summarize the key findings, statistics, and recommendations from the attached Intergovernmental Panel on Climate Change (IPCC) report in 1,000 words, highlighting points relevant to climate policy, adaptation strategies, and recent scientific updates."

How It Works

Using a tool like ChatGPT or Perplexity AI, first upload the IPCC report in PDF or Word format. Next, enter the prompt and submit. The AI will extract critical information and create a clear, chapter-ready summary, saving hours of manual reading and note-taking while ensuring no crucial details are overlooked.

6. Transforming Blog Series into a Cohesive Book Manuscript

Scenario

An author has written a 15-part blog series on mindfulness practices but needs help reorganizing it into a well-structured book.

Prompt

"Assume the role of a nonfiction author and reorganize this 15-part blog series below into a cohesive 10-chapter manuscript with logical flow, engaging chapter titles, smooth transitions, and consistent tone. Provide a suggested table of contents."

How It Works

Using a tool like ChatGPT or Gemini, first enter the prompt. Next, paste the blog series text directly below the prompt and submit. The AI will restructure the fragmented posts into a polished manuscript with unified themes and professional organization, enabling authors to efficiently transform existing content into a publishable book.

Biostatisticians

The Essential Role of a Biostatistician

Biostatisticians design, analyze, and interpret data from biomedical research, ensuring statistical rigor in clinical trials, epidemiological studies, and public health initiatives. Their work informs medical guidelines, regulatory approvals, and scientific breakthroughs.

Common Challenges Faced by Biostatisticians

Biostatisticians often face complex datasets with missing or inconsistent values, tight deadlines for interim analyses, difficulty in translating statistical results for medical stakeholders, and evolving regulatory demands.

How AI Simplifies Biostatistics Tasks

AI can automate data cleaning, perform advanced modeling, generate clear visualizations, and translate statistical outputs into stakeholder-friendly reports. Tools like ChatGPT, Gemini, Perplexity, and Microsoft Copilot help biostatisticians efficiently communicate findings and ensure timely delivery of accurate, actionable insights.

Crafting Effective Prompts for Biostatistics Tasks

This section offers practical, role-specific prompts illustrating how biostatisticians can leverage advanced AI tools like ChatGPT, Gemini, Perplexity, and Microsoft Copilot to streamline analyses, enhance clarity, and improve collaboration with clinical teams. Each example includes a realistic scenario, an optimized prompt, and a clear explanation of how AI can translate complex statistical findings into actionable, stakeholder-ready outputs.

1. Summarizing Clinical Trial Results

Scenario

A biostatistician needs to quickly prepare a summary of interim clinical trial results for a meeting with non-technical stakeholders.

> **Prompt**
> *"Act as a clinical data analyst. Using the uploaded statistical output file, summarize key findings from the interim analysis, highlighting efficacy, safety trends, and significant p-values in plain language suitable for clinicians and executives."*

How It Works

Using a tool like ChatGPT, Gemini, or Microsoft Copilot, first enter the prompt. Next, upload the statistical output file and submit. The AI will then deliver a concise, accessible summary that accurately conveys statistical outcomes.

2. Generating Data Cleaning Plans

Scenario

A biostatistician needs a structured plan to clean a dataset with missing and inconsistent patient records before analysis.

> **Prompt**
>
> *"Assume the role of a clinical data manager. Using the attached raw clinical dataset, create a step-by-step data cleaning plan addressing missing values, outliers, and formatting inconsistencies. Include justifications for each step."*

How It Works

Using a tool like ChatGPT, Gemini, or Microsoft Copilot, first enter the prompt. Next, upload the raw clinical dataset and submit. The AI will deliver a detailed cleaning strategy with clear explanations, enabling the systematic preparation of high-quality data for reliable statistical analysis and saving valuable time.

3. Drafting Statistical Analysis Plans (SAPs)

Scenario

A biostatistician needs to prepare an SAP for a Phase III oncology trial.

Prompt

"You are an experienced biostatistician. Draft a statistical analysis plan for the attached clinical trial protocol, specifying endpoints, analysis populations, methods for handling missing data, and statistical tests aligned with regulatory guidelines."

How It Works

Using a tool like ChatGPT, Gemini, or Microsoft Copilot, first enter the prompt. Next, upload the protocol document in PDF or Word format and submit. The AI will generate a professional, regulator-ready SAP outlining all statistical considerations and ensuring compliance with clinical research standards, streamlining a critical and time-intensive process.

4. Visualizing Survival Analysis Outputs

Scenario

A biostatistician needs to present Kaplan-Meier survival curves to highlight treatment differences.

Prompt

"Act as a medical statistician. Using the attached time-to-event data, generate Kaplan-Meier survival curves with median survival annotations and log-rank test results, formatted for inclusion in a clinical trial report."

How It Works

Using a tool like ChatGPT, Gemini, or Microsoft Copilot, first enter the prompt. Next, upload the time-to-event data and submit. The AI will create high-quality survival plots and statistical summaries, enabling a clear and impactful presentation of time-to-event outcomes to a wide range of stakeholders.

5. Drafting Regulatory Submission Summaries

Scenario

A biostatistician prepares a summary of statistical findings for inclusion in a New Drug Application (NDA).

Prompt

"Assume the role of a regulatory biostatistician. Using the attached final analysis report, create a concise summary of efficacy and safety results, formatted per regulatory guidelines, for submission in an NDA dossier."

How It Works

Using a tool like ChatGPT, Gemini, or Microsoft Copilot, first enter the prompt. Next, upload the final analysis report in Word or PDF and submit. The AI will generate a polished, submission-ready summary that aligns with regulatory standards, significantly streamlining the NDA preparation process and reducing the risk of manual transcription errors.

6. Checking Clinical Data Integrity for Compliance

Scenario

A biostatistician needs to ensure data integrity of a Phase II oncology trial before regulatory submission.

> **Prompt**
>
> *"You are a clinical data compliance auditor. Using the attached clinical dataset, identify inconsistencies, missing values, protocol deviations, and any outliers that could compromise data integrity. Summarize findings in a compliance report."*

How It Works

Using a tool like ChatGPT, Gemini, or Microsoft Copilot, first enter the prompt. Next, upload the clinical dataset and submit. The AI will generate a thorough integrity report detailing potential issues and actionable recommendations, helping maintain regulatory compliance and trial credibility.

Comedians

The Essential Role of a Comedian

Comedians craft and deliver humor to entertain, provoke thought, and connect with audiences. Whether through stand-up, writing, sketch comedy, or digital media, they skillfully combine timing, observation, and cultural critique to produce engaging performances that resonate across diverse audiences.

Common Challenges Faced by Comedians

Comedians often struggle with generating fresh material consistently, avoiding unintentional plagiarism, and adapting humor for different audience sensitivities. The pressure to be original, relatable, and socially aware—especially in fast-changing media spaces—adds to the creative burden.

How AI Simplifies Comedy Writing Tasks

AI tools assist comedians by brainstorming punchlines, hypothetically testing audience reactions, adjusting tone for audience demographics, and even remixing jokes into new formats. Large language models (LLMs) can rapidly prototype ideas, offer alternative phrasings, and simulate voice styles, saving time while sparking inspiration.

Crafting Effective Prompts for Comedy Tasks

This section presents practical, creative prompts designed to help comedians harness LLMs like ChatGPT and creative tools such as Invideo AI and Suno AI to generate, refine, and adapt humorous material. Each example is based on real-world comedic scenarios and includes a tested prompt along with a clear explanation of how the AI can enhance timing, tone, and originality in the writing process.

1. Punch-Up Support for a Flat Routine

Scenario

A comedian feels one section of their routine is flat and needs help adding surprise elements or sharper punchlines.

> ***Prompt***
>
> *" You are a professional comedian. Here's a paragraph from my set that needs a better payoff. Suggest three punch-up variations that enhance the surprise or absurdity. Keep the pacing consistent and punchlines concise."*

How It Works

Using a tool like ChatGPT or Gemini, first enter the prompt. Next, paste the paragraph in plain text below it and submit. The AI will analyze the rhythm, premise, and joke structure, then propose alternative punchlines with stronger comedic misdirection or exaggeration.

2. Generating Original Material from Current Events

Scenario

A stand-up comedian preparing for a weekend set wants to build a five-minute segment using this week's trending news without being offensive or repetitive.

Prompt

You are a professional stand-up *comedian. Write five original jokes based on the top three trending news headlines this week. Keep the tone witty and observational. Avoid insensitive or recycled material. Structure the jokes for a live stand-up delivery to a mixed-age audience."*

How It Works

Using a tool like ChatGPT, Perplexity AI, or Gemini, enter the prompt and submit. The AI will pull from general news context and craft original joke formats using audience-safe humor techniques. This saves time while ensuring the material stays fresh, topical, and professionally appropriate.

3. Testing Joke Variations by Tone

Scenario

A comedian is experimenting with different delivery styles (dry humor, absurdist, sarcastic) for a new routine and wants to test how tone changes the effect.

Prompt

You are an award winning comedian. Rewrite the provided joke below in three tonal variations: dry humor, absurdist, and sarcastic. Keep the setup consistent and adjust only the delivery and punchline style."

How It Works

Using a tool like ChatGPT or Gemini, first enter the prompt. Next, paste the joke or setup in plain text below it and submit. The AI will rephrase the punchline while maintaining structural integrity, showcasing how tone impacts audience reception. This helps comedians compare delivery options, improve joke adaptability, and choose styles that suit different venues or personas.

4. Building a Themed Comedy Set

Scenario

A comedian is preparing a themed 10-minute set about parenting and wants help developing interconnected material.

Prompt

"Act as internationally acclaimed comedian. Generate a 10-minute comedy set with five interconnected jokes or stories centered around parenting. Include setups, punchlines, and transitions that create narrative flow. Use a relatable tone suitable for an audience of parents aged 30–50."

How It Works

Using a tool like ChatGPT, Gemini, or Microsoft Copilot, enter the prompt and submit. The AI will generate structured, thematically cohesive jokes with smooth transitions. It blends anecdotes and observations into a set that mirrors real-life storytelling, reducing time spent developing arcs and improving audience engagement with shared experiences.

5. Short-Form Comedy Video Script with InVideo AI

Scenario

A comedian wants to quickly produce a 60-second skit about online dating mishaps for social media, using visuals, voiceover, and captions.

Prompt

"Generate a 60-second video script about online dating disasters and produce a complete video from it, including scene directions, visuals, and voiceover. Structure it for short-form platforms like TikTok or YouTube Shorts, keeping the tone light and punchy."

How It Works

Using a tool like InVideo AI, enter the prompt and submit. The AI will first draft a full script based on your request. It will then automatically generate a final video complete with relevant visuals, background music, and a professional voiceover. This single-platform workflow allows you to efficiently produce high-quality, ready-to-publish content without using multiple tools.

6. Musical Parody Writing with Suno AI

Scenario

A comedian wants to create a parody song based on a trending pop track, aimed at poking fun at gym culture and fitness fads.

Prompt

"You are a professional comedy song writer. Write a humorous parody of a pop song about gym culture and fitness obsession. Use the style of an upbeat radio hit. Include lyrics for two verses, a chorus, and a bridge. Keep it clean, catchy, and rhymed."

How It Works

This is a two-step process. Using a tool like ChatGPT or Gemini, first enter the prompt and submit to generate the full parody lyrics. Then, copy these lyrics into Suno AI, which converts them into a complete musical track, adding vocals, instrumentals, and mixing. The result is a professionally styled comedy song, ideal for reels, stand-up segues, or podcast skits.

Copywriter

Essential Role of a Copywriter

Copywriters craft persuasive, engaging content that drives action and conveys brand voice. From digital ads and product descriptions to website content and email campaigns, they transform ideas into words that sell, inform, or inspire. Their work supports marketing, sales, branding, and customer engagement across channels.

Common Challenges Faced by Copywriters

Copywriters often face tight deadlines, creative fatigue, and the need to tailor content for varied audiences and platforms. Maintaining originality while meeting client briefs and optimizing for SEO adds to the complexity of their role.

How AI Simplifies Copywriting Tasks

AI tools like ChatGPT, Gemini, and Perplexity AI support brainstorming, generate drafts, optimize headlines, adjust tone, and rewrite content for clarity or SEO. These capabilities boost productivity, spark creative direction, and allow copywriters to focus on refinement and strategy.

Crafting Effective Prompts for Copywriting Tasks

This section demonstrates how copywriters can leverage AI tools like ChatGPT, Gemini, and Perplexity AI to ideate, write, refine, and optimize marketing content across platforms. Each prompt features a real-world scenario, a strategically written prompt, and a clear explanation of how the AI tool delivers targeted, high-quality outputs aligned with copywriting objectives.

1. Writing an Attention-Grabbing Product Headline

Scenario

A copywriter is tasked with crafting a headline for a new eco-friendly detergent brand targeting environmentally conscious millennials.

> ***Prompt***
>
> *"You are a creative copywriter. Write five punchy, benefit-driven headline options for a new eco-friendly detergent brand targeting millennials. Highlight sustainability, effectiveness, and clean scent appeal."*

How It Works

Using a tool like ChatGPT or Gemini, first, enter the prompt and then, submit. The AI instantly generates multiple headline variations with a tone, structure, and word choice tailored to resonate with the intended demographic and value proposition. This is ideal for quickly brainstorming and A/B testing.

2. Generating Website Copy for a Product Landing Page

Scenario

A freelance copywriter is developing website content for a startup that's launching a new AI-powered scheduling app designed for remote teams. The copy must be engaging, benefit-oriented, and optimized for conversions.

Prompt

"You are a SaaS copywriter. Write compelling (150-word) landing page copy for a new AI-powered scheduling app designed for remote teams. Emphasize time-saving, integration with existing calendars, ease of use, and benefits for distributed teams."

How It Works

Using a tool like ChatGPT or Gemini, first, enter the prompt and then, submit. The AI generates persuasive, structured landing page copy highlighting key features and emotional benefits. The output typically includes a headline, subheading, product benefits, and a clear call to action—all crafted to boost user engagement and drive sign-ups.

3. Writing a Series of Promotional Emails for a Product Launch

Scenario

A copywriter is hired to create an email sequence for the launch of a new online course teaching small business owners how to build an effective brand identity. The campaign needs to build anticipation, introduce the course, and drive conversions.

> ***Prompt***
>
> *"You are an experienced email marketing copywriter. Write a 3-part promotional email sequence for the launch of a new course titled 'Build Your Brand Blueprint.' Target busy small business owners. Each email should include a compelling subject line, engaging introduction, and persuasive call to action. Emphasize pain points, transformation, and urgency."*

How It Works

Using a tool like ChatGPT, Perplexity AI, or Gemini, first, enter the prompt and then, submit. The AI will generate three distinct but connected emails, each tailored to guide readers through the awareness, interest, and decision phases. The result is a ready-to-use sequence designed to boost course sign-ups and engagement.

4. Crafting Product Descriptions for an E-Commerce Store

Scenario

A freelance copywriter is tasked with writing compelling product descriptions for a new collection of handcrafted leather bags, aimed at eco-conscious professionals shopping online.

Prompt

"You are an e-commerce copywriter. Write three unique product descriptions (100–120 words each) for a line of handcrafted, eco-friendly leather bags targeting environmentally conscious professionals. Highlight sustainability, craftsmanship, functional design, and professional appeal. Each description should include an attention-grabbing headline, feature-benefit structure, and persuasive tone."

How It Works

Using a tool like ChatGPT or Gemini, first, enter the prompt and then, submit. The AI returns three tailored product descriptions that balance vivid storytelling with strategic selling points. By aligning with the target audience's values and lifestyle, the output enhances product appeal, supports brand consistency, and increases the likelihood of conversion.

5. Repurposing Long-Form Content into Multi-Platform Snippets

Scenario

A copywriter wants to repurpose a 2,000-word blog post into multiple short-form content assets for digital channels.

Prompt

"You are a content strategist. Repurpose the blog post below into:

a 150-word LinkedIn post,

a 70-word Instagram caption,

a 60-word Facebook teaser, and

a 30-word email preview.

Maintain the original message but adapt each version for its respective platform's audience and tone."

[Paste blog post here]

How It Works

Using a tool like ChatGPT, Perplexity AI, or Gemini, first enter the prompt. Next, paste the full blog post directly below it and submit. The AI extracts key messages and reshapes them into format-specific, attention-grabbing snippets. This saves significant time and ensures content remains consistent yet customized for each digital platform.

6. Crafting Copy for a Limited-Time Offer Campaign

Scenario

A copywriter is preparing promotional content for an e-commerce store launching a 72-hour flash sale on eco-friendly kitchenware.

> ***Prompt***
>
> *"You are an e-commerce copywriter. Write compelling homepage banner copy (max 30 words), a 100-word promotional email, and a 60-word social media caption for a 72-hour flash sale on eco-friendly kitchenware. Emphasize urgency, sustainability, and the 40% discount, and use persuasive language tailored to environmentally conscious shoppers."*

How It Works

Using a tool like ChatGPT, Gemini, or Microsoft Copilot, first, enter this multi-part prompt and then, submit. The AI generates channel-optimized marketing copy that aligns with the campaign's tone, urgency, and values. It helps copywriters efficiently create cohesive messaging across different platforms while preserving clarity and impact.

Cybersecurity Specialist

Essential Role of a Cybersecurity Specialist

Cybersecurity specialists safeguard digital assets by identifying vulnerabilities, implementing security protocols, and monitoring systems for threats. They conduct risk assessments, enforce compliance standards, and respond to breaches to maintain confidentiality, integrity, and availability across information systems.

Common Challenges Faced by Cybersecurity Specialists

Cybersecurity professionals contend with evolving threat landscapes, resource constraints, and complex regulatory requirements. Balancing proactive defense with incident response, managing zero-day vulnerabilities, and ensuring secure user behavior remain persistent challenges.

How AI Simplifies Cybersecurity Tasks

AI platforms like ChatGPT, Perplexity AI, Microsoft Copilot, and Gemini aid cybersecurity tasks by automating threat detection, summarizing logs, drafting incident reports, and analyzing compliance gaps. These tools support real-time responses, reduce manual workload, and enhance threat intelligence.

Crafting Effective Prompts for Cybersecurity Tasks

This section presents role-specific prompts tailored to typical responsibilities in cybersecurity. Each prompt simulates real-world scenarios and is designed for platforms such as ChatGPT, Perplexity, Microsoft Copilot or Gemini. With structured input, cybersecurity professionals can accelerate risk analysis, automate routine reporting, and ensure regulatory alignment.

1. Threat Intelligence Summary from Logs

Scenario

A cybersecurity specialist needs to quickly identify anomalies and summarize potential risks from vast amounts of daily system and firewall logs.

> ***Prompt***
>
> *"You are a cybersecurity analyst. Analyze the following logs below to identify potential threats, anomalies, and indicators of compromise. Summarize key findings and recommend follow-up actions."*

How It Works

Using a tool like ChatGPT, Perplexity, or Gemini, first enter the prompt. Next, paste the raw logs directly below it and submit. The AI will scan the data to extract unusual behavior, flag known threat patterns, and summarize insights into a digestible threat report.

2. Security Policy Drafting for New Infrastructure

Scenario

A cybersecurity specialist needs to draft a comprehensive security policy for a newly deployed cloud infrastructure, including access controls, encryption standards, and incident response procedures.

> ***Prompt***
>
> *"You are a cybersecurity policy advisor. Draft a comprehensive security policy for the cloud infrastructure described below. Include access control, encryption, data backup, threat monitoring, and incident response guidelines."*

How It Works

Using a tool like ChatGPT, Gemini, or Perplexity, first enter the prompt. Next, paste a detailed description of the cloud infrastructure, including services used, user roles, data types, and regulatory obligations, directly below it and submit. The AI will tailor a detailed policy that aligns with cybersecurity governance best practices, enabling consistent enforcement and audit readiness.

3. Threat Modeling for a Web Application

Scenario

A cybersecurity specialist is conducting a threat modeling exercise for a new web application and must identify potential attack vectors, assess vulnerabilities, and prioritize mitigations.

> ***Prompt***
>
> *"You are a cybersecurity analyst. Conduct a threat model for the web application described below. Identify potential attack vectors, assess risk severity, and recommend mitigation strategies using frameworks like STRIDE or DREAD."*

How It Works

Using a tool like ChatGPT or Gemini, first enter the prompt. Next, paste key details about the web application architecture, data flow, authentication methods, and user roles directly below it and submit. The AI will generate a structured threat model, including categorized risks and mitigation recommendations. This supports secure design decisions and regulatory compliance.

4. Cloud Security Risk Assessment

Scenario

A cybersecurity specialist is evaluating the security posture for a company planning to migrate sensitive workloads to a public cloud platform.

> ***Prompt***
>
> *"You are a cloud security analyst. Based on the context below, conduct a cloud security risk assessment. Identify potential threats, vulnerabilities, and recommend mitigation strategies aligned with best practices (e.g., encryption, IAM, monitoring)."*

How It Works

Using a tool like ChatGPT, Gemini, or Perplexity, first enter the prompt. Next, paste the planned cloud environment details (e.g., AWS, Azure), workload type, compliance needs, and migration goals directly below it and submit. The AI will generate a risk profile with mitigation actions, supporting informed cloud security decisions and ensuring regulatory and operational readiness.

5. Security Incident Classification and Escalation Mapping

Scenario

A cybersecurity analyst must categorize incoming security alerts based on severity and define appropriate escalation pathways for their team.

> ***Prompt***
>
> *"You are a cybersecurity operations analyst. Classify the following security incidents below by severity level (low, medium, high, critical) and map each to an appropriate escalation path, including responsible teams, response timelines, and communication protocols."*

How It Works

Using a tool like ChatGPT or Gemini, first enter the prompt. Next, paste a list or log of security incidents, including timestamps, event types, and initial indicators, directly below it and submit. The AI will evaluate incident context, apply risk categorization logic, and output a structured escalation matrix that supports rapid response and governance compliance.

6. Cybersecurity Strategy Roadmap Development

Scenario

A Chief Information Security Officer (CISO) needs to develop a one-year cybersecurity roadmap that aligns security initiatives with evolving business goals and threat landscapes.

> ***Prompt***
>
> *"You are a cybersecurity strategist. Develop a one-year cybersecurity roadmap for the organization described below. Align the plan with business objectives, threat trends, compliance needs, and emerging technologies. Include key initiatives, milestones, timelines, and responsible roles."*

How It Works

Using a tool like ChatGPT or Gemini, first enter the prompt. Next, paste organizational context, such as industry, size, existing security posture, known threats, and strategic goals, directly below it and submit. The AI synthesizes the input to produce a detailed, milestone-based roadmap outlining proactive initiatives. This helps security leaders communicate vision, prioritize resources, and demonstrate alignment with business resilience objectives.

Data Analysts

The Essential Role of a Data Analyst

Data analysts transform raw data into actionable insights, driving informed decision-making across industries. They clean, organize, and interpret complex datasets to identify trends, measure performance, and communicate findings through reports, dashboards, or visualizations that inform business strategy.

Common Challenges Faced by Data Analysts

Data analysts frequently juggle messy datasets, unclear stakeholder requirements, tight deadlines, and the need to translate technical findings into plain language for diverse audiences. Ensuring data accuracy, aligning analyses with business goals, and effectively visualizing results remain constant pressures.

How AI Simplifies Data Analysis Tasks

AI assists data analysts by automating data cleaning, generating summaries, drafting reports, and suggesting visualizations. Large language models (LLMs) rapidly produce executive summaries, rephrase technical content for stakeholders, or script code for analysis—accelerating workflows while improving clarity and efficiency.

Crafting Effective Prompts for Data Analysis Tasks

This section provides practical prompts tailored to help data analysts leverage LLMs like ChatGPT, Gemini, and Microsoft Copilot to accelerate data preparation, analysis, and reporting. Each example presents a realistic scenario, an effective prompt, and a brief explanation of how AI enhances data-driven workflows.

1. Exploratory Data Summary

Scenario

A data analyst needs a quick overview of a new sales dataset before a deeper analysis.

> **Prompt**
>
> *"Summarize the attached sales dataset, highlighting key statistics such as mean, median, mode, missing values, outliers, and basic trends across date, region, and product lines."*

How It Works

Using a tool like ChatGPT or Gemini, first upload your dataset in Excel or CSV format. Next, enter the prompt and submit. The AI scans the data, calculates descriptive statistics, detects outliers, and identifies trends, helping analysts quickly understand data structure and plan next steps.

2. Data Cleaning Strategy Draft

Scenario

A data analyst needs to plan a data cleaning strategy for a dataset with inconsistent date formats and duplicate entries.

> **Prompt**
>
> *"You are a professional data analyst. Draft a step-by-step data cleaning plan for the attached dataset, focusing on resolving inconsistent date formats, removing duplicates, and standardizing categorical variables. Explain each step clearly."*

How It Works

Using a tool like ChatGPT or Gemini, first upload your problematic dataset in Excel or CSV format. Next, enter the prompt and submit. The AI analyzes data quality issues and outputs a detailed, practical cleaning plan, saving time and ensuring reproducible preprocessing for analysis or modeling.

3. Insightful Executive Summary

Scenario

A data analyst needs to present complex sales performance metrics to executives in a brief, accessible summary.

Prompt

"Write a 200-word executive summary of Q3 sales performance, based on the attached dataset. Highlight key metrics, regional differences, top products, and actionable insights, using clear, non-technical language."

How it Works

Using a tool like ChatGPT, Microsoft Copilot, or Gemini, first upload your dataset. Next, enter the prompt and submit. The AI distills complex metrics into a concise summary tailored for non-technical leaders, improving communication efficiency and supporting confident decision-making.

4. Revenue Distribution Chart by Region

Scenario

A senior financial analyst needs to visualize regional revenue performance for a strategic planning meeting.

> **Prompt**
>
> *"Act as a senior financial analyst. Analyze the attached revenue dataset and generate a bar chart comparing total revenue by region for the last fiscal year. Highlight the top three regions in distinct colors for clarity."*

How It Works

Using a tool like ChatGPT, Microsoft Copilot, or Gemini, first upload the dataset. Next, enter the prompt and submit. The AI processes the data and generates a color-coded bar chart, facilitating data-driven discussions on regional business performance.

5. Monthly Customer Churn Heatmap

Scenario

A customer insights specialist wants to identify seasonal churn trends for targeted retention campaigns.

Prompt

"Act as a customer insights specialist. Using the attached churn dataset, produce a heatmap of monthly customer churn rates over the past two years, emphasizing peak churn months with a red gradient."

How It Works

Using a tool like ChatGPT or Gemini, first upload your churn data. Next, enter the prompt and submit. The AI calculates monthly churn rates and produces an intuitive heatmap, enabling quick identification of seasonal churn spikes for strategic retention efforts.

6. Product Category Performance Pie Chart

Scenario

A business intelligence analyst needs a clear visual for an executive meeting showing revenue breakdown by product line.

Prompt

"Act as a business intelligence analyst. From the provided sales dataset below, create a pie chart illustrating revenue share by product category for the past year. Include clear labels and percentages."

How It Works

Using a tool like ChatGPT or Gemini, first enter the prompt. Next, paste your sales dataset directly below it and submit. The AI calculates revenue shares by category and generates a labeled pie chart presenting data clearly for executive decision-makers.

Designers

The Essential Role of a Designer

Designers transform ideas into compelling visuals that communicate messages effectively across print, digital, and product platforms. By blending creativity with functionality, they craft user-centered solutions that elevate brands and engage audiences.

Common Challenges Faced by Designers

Designers face hurdles aligning concepts to client expectations, tight deadlines, creative block, and repeated revisions. Balancing aesthetics with usability and clearly communicating design intent to non-design stakeholders are frequent obstacles.

How AI Simplifies Design Tasks

AI streamlines ideation by generating design variations, resizing assets, drafting social posts, and enhancing consistency. This accelerates workflows, freeing designers to focus on creativity while ensuring brand cohesion across deliverables.

Crafting Effective Prompts for Design Tasks

This section provides practical prompts tailored to help designers leverage AI tools like ChatGPT, Gemini, Midjourney, Canva AI, and Leonardo AI. These examples show how to generate fresh concepts, enhance branding, streamline visual production, and improve design communication. Each scenario includes a realistic use case, an optimized prompt, and a clear explanation of how AI supports creativity and efficiency.

1. Generating Logo Concepts

Scenario

A designer needs to generate initial logo concepts for a sustainable skincare brand.

> **Prompt**
>
> *"Act as a creative director. Generate three minimalist logo concepts for an eco-friendly skincare brand, using earthy tones and nature-inspired elements. Provide a brief rationale for each concept."*

How It Works

Using a tool like ChatGPT, Gemini, or Canva AI , enter the prompt and submit. The AI will generate minimalist logo ideas with explanations, accelerating ideation and providing designers with clear directions to develop concepts with clients.

2. Luxury Watch Ad Visual

Scenario

A creative team needs a sophisticated hero image for a luxury timepiece campaign.

Prompt

"Render a high-end wristwatch displayed on dark marble, illuminated by a dramatic spotlight to emphasize its brushed steel case. Incorporate subtle reflections to highlight craftsmanship, with a minimalist background for a refined, editorial look."

How It Works

Using a tool like Leonardo AI, Canva AI, or Gemini, enter the prompt and submit. The AI will produce photorealistic visuals suitable for luxury advertising and editorial marketing materials.

3. Evening Gown Concept Sketch

Scenario

A fashion designer wants a glamorous sketch of a flowing evening gown for a couture collection proposal.

> **Prompt**
>
> *"Illustrate a floor-length evening gown with a deep emerald satin fabric, plunging neckline, and delicate silver embroidery. Show the dress on a runway model, capturing movement and luxurious texture."*

How It Works

Using a tool like Midjourney, Leonardo AI, Canva AI, or Gemini, enter the prompt and submit. The AI generates elegant fashion concept art, helping designers communicate design intent effectively to clients or stakeholders.

4. Product Concept Render: Ergonomic Office Chair

Scenario

A product designer wants to visualize an ergonomic office chair concept for a new workspace furniture line.

Prompt

"Render an ergonomic office chair with breathable mesh, adjustable lumbar support, sleek black frame, and minimalist silhouette. Showcase the chair in a modern office environment with natural light and subtle background props."

How It Works

Using a tool like Leonardo AI, Canva AI, or Gemini, enter the prompt and submit. The AI produces photorealistic renders perfect for client presentations, marketing collateral, and design approvals.

5. Exploded View of Gadget Design

Scenario

A designer needs a clear exploded-view diagram of a compact portable blender for assembly instructions.

Prompt

"Create a detailed exploded-view illustration of a portable blender, showing motor base, blade assembly, detachable cup, and lid components, labeled clearly against a white background."

How It Works

Using a tool like Gemini, Canva AI, Midjourney, or Leonardo AI, enter the prompt and submit. The AI generates high-resolution exploded-view visuals optimized for user manuals, manufacturing documentation, or patent applications.

6. Textile Pattern Variations

Scenario

A fashion designer needs fresh patterns for a summer dress line targeting young adults.

Prompt

"Generate four seamless textile patterns featuring playful floral and geometric designs in a pastel color palette suitable for summer dresses, ensuring high-resolution and repeatability for fabric printing."

How It Works

Using a tool like Gemini, Canva AI, or Leonardo AI, first enter the prompt and submit. The AI will create editable, scalable textile pattern files ready for sampling, production, or mood boards.

Economists

The Essential Role of an Economist

Economists analyze data to understand, forecast, and influence economic trends, informing policies, investment strategies, and organizational decisions. Their insights shape monetary policy, labor markets, and global trade.

Common Challenges Faced by Economists

Economists face challenges like processing massive datasets, integrating disparate economic indicators, modeling complex relationships, and effectively communicating forecasts to diverse audiences under tight deadlines.

How AI Simplifies Economic Tasks

AI tools streamline time-intensive processes, automate data aggregation, detect trends in complex datasets, and generate clear economic narratives. Tools like ChatGPT, Gemini, Perplexity, and Microsoft Copilot assist with drafting detailed reports, building econometric models, and visualizing scenarios—empowering economists to deliver timely, accurate insights.

Crafting Effective Prompts for Economic Tasks

This section provides practical, role-specific prompts to help economists harness the power of AI tools such as ChatGPT, Gemini, Perplexity, and Microsoft Copilot. These examples demonstrate how to craft effective prompts for complex economic analyses, data visualization, policy evaluation, and market forecasting. Each prompt includes a realistic scenario, a precisely optimized prompt, and a clear explanation of how AI can accelerate workflows and produce actionable economic insights.

1. Summarizing Economic Indicators Brief

Scenario

An economist needs to quickly brief executives on recent economic data, including GDP, unemployment, and inflation.

> **Prompt**
> *"You are a macroeconomic analyst. Using the attached dataset, draft a 450-word summary highlighting recent GDP, unemployment, and inflation trends with key policy implications."*

How It Works

Using a tool like ChatGPT, Gemini, or Microsoft Copilot, first upload the dataset in a format like docx, csv, xlsx, or json. Next, enter the prompt and submit. The AI will analyze the data and produce a concise, executive-ready summary emphasizing important economic trends and policy impacts.

2. Building Inflation Forecast Models

Scenario

An economist needs to forecast inflation for the next five years based on macroeconomic indicators.

> ***Prompt***
>
> *"Act as an economic forecaster. Using the attached time-series data, build a predictive model estimating annual inflation for the next five years. Include clear line charts showing forecasted inflation with confidence intervals and label key inflection points."*

How It Works

Using a tool like ChatGPT, Gemini, or Microsoft Copilot, first upload the macroeconomic dataset in a format like docx, csv, xlsx, or json. Next, enter the prompt and submit. The AI will generate a visual-rich forecast report with annotated charts that clearly communicate projections and economic drivers for stakeholder presentation.

3. Evaluating Fiscal Policy Impacts

Scenario

An economist must assess how proposed tax changes will affect key economic indicators like GDP, employment, and household income.

> **Prompt**
>
> *"You are a fiscal policy analyst. Using the attached economic model assumptions, evaluate the projected impacts of proposed tax changes on GDP, employment, and household income, providing a comprehensive 1,500-word report suitable for policymakers."*

How it Works

Using a tool like ChatGPT, Gemini, or Microsoft Copilot, first upload the economic model assumptions file. Next, enter the prompt and submit. The AI will produce a detailed, policy-focused report with clear explanations and scenario comparisons to aid evidence-based decision-making.

4. Generating Comparative Country Economic Profiles

Scenario

An economist needs to compare key indicators across multiple countries for an international briefing.

Prompt

"Act as an international economist. Research and summarize GDP growth, inflation, and unemployment rates for at least five countries in West Africa. Provide a comparative profile with side-by-side bar charts or tables highlighting significant differences and trends."

How it Works

Using a tool like Perplexity AI or Gemini, first enter the prompt and submit. The AI will produce a clear, visually-supported comparative report featuring interpretable charts and concise summaries that elucidate cross-country economic distinctions for stakeholders.

5. Comparing Historical Recessions Across Major Economies

Scenario

An economist wants to compare how the U.S., EU, and China navigated the 2008 financial crisis and the 2020 COVID-19 recession.

Prompt

"You are a macroeconomic historian. Research and compare the 2008 financial crisis and the 2020 COVID-19 recession across the U.S., EU, and China. Summarize differences in causes, policy responses, recovery paths, and long-term economic impacts in a 1,500-word report."

How It Works

Using a tool like Perplexity AI or Gemini, first enter the prompt and submit. The AI will deliver a thorough comparative analysis highlighting how major economies managed each crisis, providing valuable insights for policy analysis and investment decisions.

6. Generating Global Economic Outlook Briefs

Scenario

An economist needs to brief executives on upcoming growth forecasts across G20 countries.

Prompt

"Act as an international economic forecaster. Research and summarize current GDP growth forecasts, inflation trends, and key economic risks for G20 nations. Highlight regional differences and global themes in a 500-word briefing."

How It Works

Using a tool like Perplexity AI or Gemini, first enter the prompt and submit. The AI will generate a concise, data-driven global economic outlook delivering timely, accurate insights for executive decision-making without manual data collection.

Epidemiologist

Essential Role of an Epidemiologist

Epidemiologists investigate the patterns, causes, and effects of diseases within populations. They design and conduct studies, analyze data to track outbreaks, assess risk factors, and inform public health policies. Their work guides interventions that reduce disease burden and improve population health outcomes.

Common Challenges Faced by Epidemiologists

Epidemiologists often deal with data incompleteness, underreporting, evolving pathogens, and political or logistical barriers during outbreaks. Rapid response demands, interdisciplinary coordination, and communicating findings to non-experts further complicate their role.

How AI Simplifies Epidemiological Tasks

AI tools like Perplexity AI, ChatGPT, and Gemini assist epidemiologists by automating data extraction, forecasting trends, mapping transmission networks, and generating reports. These platforms help synthesize vast datasets and improve the speed, clarity, and precision of epidemiological analysis.

Crafting Effective Prompts for Epidemiological Tasks

This section presents strategically crafted prompts aligned with the analytical and communicative tasks performed by epidemiologists. Each prompt models a real-world public health scenario and is optimized for platforms such as ChatGPT, Gemini, and Perplexity. By mastering prompt design, epidemiologists can accelerate data analysis, enhance surveillance reporting, and improve decision-making in public health responses.

1. Generating a Summary of Disease Surveillance Data

Scenario

An epidemiologist needs to summarize weekly disease surveillance data for internal reporting.

Prompt

"You are an epidemiologist. Summarize the disease surveillance data provided below into a brief report highlighting trends, anomalies, and priority areas for further investigation."

How It Works

Using a tool like ChatGPT or Perplexity, first enter the prompt. Next, paste the surveillance data (e.g., in a docx, csv or xlsx table format) directly below it and submit. The AI will analyze and organize patterns, drafting a concise report that highlights key findings and areas requiring attention.

2. Mapping a Disease Outbreak Using Case Data

Scenario

An epidemiologist is analyzing a recent disease outbreak and needs to generate a preliminary transmission map to identify clusters and potential sources of exposure.

> ***Prompt***
>
> *"You are a field epidemiologist. Using the case data provided below, identify geographic clusters and likely transmission paths. Suggest visual formats for a basic transmission or heat map."*

How It Works

Using a tool like ChatGPT or Gemini, first enter the prompt. Next, paste the complete case dataset (e.g., in a docx, csv, or xlsx table format) directly below it and submit. The AI will analyze spatiotemporal patterns, detect clusters, and recommend suitable visualization formats to support outbreak response.

3. Drafting a Public Health Advisory for Measles Outbreak.

Scenario

An epidemiologist must create an advisory following a major measles outbreak.

> ***Prompt***
>
> *"You are a public health epidemiologist. Compose a timely advisory addressing the 2025 measles outbreak. Include transmission routes, clinical signs, vaccination recommendations, and guidance for outbreak control."*

How It Works

Using a tool like ChatGPT or Perplexity AI, enter the prompt and submit. The AI will generate a clear, evidence-based public advisory outlining risk factors, vaccination urgency, and community prevention measures.

4. Evaluating Public Health Intervention Effectiveness

Scenario

An epidemiologist is assessing the impact of a six-month community-based malaria prevention program.

> ***Prompt***
>
> *You are a public health epidemiologist. Evaluate the effectiveness of the malaria intervention program using the provided data. Identify outcome trends, implementation gaps, and recommendations for scaling or revising the program.*

How It Works

Using a tool like ChatGPT, Perplexity AI, or Gemini, first upload the full dataset in a format like docx, csv, or xlsx. Next, enter the prompt and submit. The AI will compare baseline and follow-up indicators, highlight statistically significant trends, and provide structured insights on intervention success or shortcomings to guide data-driven program decisions.

5. Detecting Health Misinformation Trends Online

Scenario

An epidemiologist wants to monitor and counteract vaccine misinformation spreading on social media platforms.

> ***Prompt***
>
> *"You are a public health data analyst. Analyze the following social media excerpts below to identify emerging vaccine misinformation trends. Summarize themes, origin patterns, and potential public health risks."*

How It Works

Using a tool like ChatGPT or Perplexity AI, first enter the prompt. Next, paste anonymized social media excerpts, hashtags, or post samples directly below it and submit. The AI will detect misinformation patterns, cluster sentiment, and suggest targeted communication strategies to help preempt and counter misinformation campaigns effectively.

6. Generating a Summary of Epidemiological Research

Scenario

An epidemiologist needs to quickly understand key findings from a complex research paper to inform a team meeting.

> ***Prompt***
>
> *"You are an epidemiological researcher. Summarize the key findings, methodology, and limitations of the attached research paper on COVID-19 transmission dynamics. Focus on results relevant to public health policy."*

How It Works

Using a tool like ChatGPT, Gemini, or Perplexity, first upload the research paper in a format like pdf or docx. Next, enter the prompt and submit. The AI will analyze the document and provide a concise, focused summary that saves time and ensures key insights inform policymaking discussions.

Filmmakers

The Essential Role of a Filmmaker

Filmmakers orchestrate creative, technical, and logistical elements to transform scripts into compelling visual narratives. Their responsibilities span directing, cinematography, editing, and production management, uniting artistic vision with practical execution.

Common Challenges Faced by Filmmakers

Filmmakers often grapple with tight budgets, compressed timelines, creative blocks, and the need for meticulous previsualization. Managing large teams and coordinating complex shoots amplify these difficulties.

How AI Simplifies Filmmaking Tasks

AI tools streamline pre-production visualization, automate script breakdowns, and enhance editing. Cuebric AI assists with cinematic scene generation; InVideo creates storyboards or trailers from text; ChatGPT and Gemini draft scripts or refine dialogue, enabling filmmakers to ideate, plan, and execute projects faster with fewer resources.

Crafting Effective Prompts for Filmmaking Tasks

This section demonstrates how filmmakers can harness AI tools such as Cuebric, InVideo, ChatGPT, Canva AI, and Gemini to elevate every stage of production—from scriptwriting and visual development to editing and marketing materials. Each example prompt features a realistic scenario, an optimized request tailored to creative workflows, and a clear explanation of how AI streamlines complex filmmaking tasks, helping professionals translate ideas into polished visual content with greater speed and precision.

1. Tense Dialogue Exchange

Scenario

A screenwriter wants a fiery confrontation revealing secrets for a script.

> ***Prompt***
>
> *"You are an award-winning screenwriter. Write a 150-word heated argument between two rival homicide detectives in a precinct office, where one accuses the other of tampering with evidence to sabotage a case."*

How It Works

Using a tool like ChatGPT or Gemini, first enter the prompt. Next, submit. The AI will produce a gripping, professionally crafted dialogue that emphasizes conflict and tension, ideal for screenplay development.

2. Crafting a Compelling Script Synopsis

Scenario

A screenwriter needs a gripping one-paragraph synopsis for a psychological thriller.

Prompt

"You are a professional screenwriter. Write a 150-word synopsis for a psychological thriller about a detective haunted by visions of his unsolved cases, exploring themes of guilt, obsession, and blurred reality."

How It Works

Using a tool like ChatGPT or Gemini, first enter the prompt. Next, submit. The AI will generate a concise, suspenseful synopsis that captures the tone, stakes, and character dynamics, suited for pitching or funding applications.

3. Directing Scene Shot Lists

Scenario

A director needs to plan a tense, climactic courtroom scene and needs a thorough shot list for their cinematography team.

Prompt

"You are an experienced film director. Create a comprehensive shot list for a five-minute courtroom showdown scene where a defense attorney exposes a key witness's lies. Include suggested camera angles, lenses, lighting notes, and emotional beats to emphasize character reactions, shifting power dynamics, and tension-building moments."

How It Works

Using a tool like ChatGPT or Gemini, first enter the prompt. Next, submit. The AI will deliver an organized, professional-quality shot list that guides camera setups, visual storytelling, and mood shifts to ensure an impactful sequence.

4. Creating Cinematic Background Plates

Scenario

A filmmaker wants a photorealistic environment for a virtual production and needs a misty mountain range at sunrise to set an epic tone.

Prompt

"Generate a 2.5D cinematic background of a misty mountain range at sunrise with dramatic lighting, suitable for an epic fantasy film's opening scene."

How It Works

Using a tool like Cuebric AI, Invideo AI, or Midjourney, first enter the prompt. Next, submit. The AI will create a high-resolution 2.5D background with depth segmentation, ready for virtual production or Unreal Engine integration, enabling immersive environment visualization.

5. Previsualizing Action Sequences

Scenario

A filmmaker needs a storyboard for a complex car chase scene to communicate vision with the stunt team.

Prompt

"Generate a six-frame storyboard illustrating a nighttime city car chase with varied camera angles, including overhead shots, close-ups, and dynamic tracking perspectives."

How It Works

Using a tool like Cuebric AI, Gemini, or Canva AI, first enter the prompt. Next, submit. The AI will generate sequential cinematic storyboard frames showing key moments, camera placements, and movement directions to help plan stunts, pacing, and creative alignment.

6. Crafting a Social Media Trailer

Scenario

A director needs a 45-second teaser video to promote a new indie film on social media platforms like Instagram or TikTok.

Prompt

"Create a 45-second cinematic trailer for an indie romance film, using the following script excerpt below. Include upbeat music, dynamic transitions, and subtitle overlays."

How It Works

Using a tool like InVideo AI, first enter the prompt. Next, paste your script excerpt from a text-based file (.txt, .docx) directly below it, and submit. The AI will automatically produce a polished teaser video with synchronized visuals, upbeat music, and text animations, which is ideal for social media campaigns.

Journalist

The Essential Role of a Journalist

Journalists investigate, analyze, and communicate timely information to inform the public, holding institutions accountable and shaping societal understanding. Their work ranges from breaking news coverage and feature writing to in-depth investigative reporting. Accuracy, clarity, and ethical standards are central to their role, as is the ability to distill complex topics into accessible narratives.

Common Challenges Faced by Journalists

Journalists often face tight deadlines, information overload, and verifying sources under pressure. They must condense large volumes of data into concise stories while avoiding misinformation. Balancing objectivity with engaging storytelling adds further complexity, especially when covering controversial or nuanced issues.

How AI Simplifies Journalism Tasks

AI can automate research, draft initial story outlines, summarize long documents, and generate data-driven visualizations. Tools like Perplexity AI excel in fact-finding, while ChatGPT and Gemini assist with crafting polished, coherent articles faster.

Crafting Effective Prompts for Journalism Tasks

This section presents hands-on, profession-specific prompts to help journalists harness AI tools like ChatGPT, Gemini, Canva AI, and Perplexity AI for faster, more accurate, and engaging reporting. Each prompt includes a realistic scenario, a targeted prompt, and a clear explanation of how it works, enabling journalists to streamline research, draft compelling stories, and enhance audience impact.

1. Summarizing Complex Reports

Scenario

A journalist needs to quickly condense a 50-page government report into a 300-word summary for a breaking news article.

> **Prompt**
>
> *You are an investigative journalist. Summarize the attached government report into a 300-word news brief highlighting key findings, statistics, and policy implications.*

How It Works

Using a tool like ChatGPT, Gemini, or Perplexity AI, first upload the report as a PDF or Word document. Next, enter the prompt and submit. The AI will analyze the document, extracting essential details and producing a concise, accurate summary tailored for fast-paced newsroom requirements.

2. Generating Interview Questions

Scenario

A journalist needs sharp, insightful interview questions for a feature on a climate scientist.

> **Prompt**
>
> *"You are a senior science reporter. Generate 12 thoughtful, open-ended interview questions for a feature on Dr. [insert name], a leading climate scientist. Questions should cover recent research findings, climate policy views, personal motivations, and advice for young scientists."*

How it Works

Using a tool like ChatGPT or Gemini, first enter the prompt, inserting the scientist's name. For enhanced accuracy, optionally upload or paste the scientist's recent papers as PDF or text files. Next, submit. The AI will craft a curated list of insightful questions to support effective interviews and compelling storytelling.

3. Analyzing Public Opinion on Breaking News

Scenario

A journalist covering a sudden government policy announcement needs a quick analysis of social media sentiment to gauge public reaction.

Prompt

"You are a data journalist. Analyze recent tweets and public comments about [insert policy/event] from the past 48 hours. Identify key themes, overall sentiment, and notable quotes representing diverse perspectives. Summarize findings in 300 words with bullet points highlighting contrasting views."

How It Works

Using a tool like ChatGPT, Gemini, or Perplexity AI, first enter the prompt. Optionally, you can upload collected social media data as CSV or text files. Next, submit. The AI will analyze patterns, sentiment trends, and key themes, delivering a clear, balanced overview for real-time integration into news stories.

4. Creating Data-Driven Visual Summaries

Scenario

A journalist covering income inequality needs to visualize recent statistics for an online article.

Prompt

"You are an investigative data reporter. Using the attached income distribution dataset, create three clear charts: a bar chart comparing income brackets, a line chart showing trends over the last decade, and a pie chart depicting income share by population segments. Include brief layman's explanations for each chart."

How It Works

Using a tool like ChatGPT, Gemini, or Perplexity AI, first upload the dataset in CSV or Excel format. Next, enter the prompt and submit. The AI generates publication-ready, well-labeled charts with jargon-free explanations, making complex data accessible to readers and enhancing article engagement.

5. Writing Compelling Story Leads

Scenario

A journalist is writing a human-interest feature on a local community rebuilding after a natural disaster and needs a gripping opening paragraph.

Prompt

"You are a feature writer for a national newspaper. Write a 100-word opening paragraph for a story on [insert community name] rebuilding after [insert disaster], focusing on emotional storytelling, vivid imagery, and a strong hook to capture readers."

How It Works

Using a tool like ChatGPT, Gemini, or Perplexity AI, first enter the prompt and submit. For best results, provide a brief context summary or bullet points outlining key disaster impacts and recovery details. The AI will craft an evocative, engaging lead, setting a compelling tone for the feature.

6. Drafting Multimedia Content Plans

Scenario

A journalist needs a plan for integrating text, video, and interactive elements into an online feature on urban housing crises.

Prompt

"You are a multimedia editor. Develop a detailed content plan for an online feature on [insert topic, e.g., urban housing crises], outlining placements for videos, interactive charts, photo galleries, and data visualizations to maximize reader engagement and narrative flow."

How It Works

Using a tool like ChatGPT, Gemini, or Canva AI, first enter the prompt, specifying the topic. Next, submit. The AI will produce a section-by-section multimedia content plan specifying optimal placements and explaining how each element complements the story, enhancing audience understanding of complex issues.

HR Managers

The Essential Role of an HR Manager

HR Managers oversee recruitment, employee relations, training, and performance management, ensuring organizations attract, develop, and retain top talent. They foster positive workplace cultures, resolve conflicts, and maintain compliance with labor laws, balancing organizational goals with employee well-being.

Common Challenges Faced by HR Managers

HR managers often face time-consuming resume screening, coordinating training programs, resolving complex conflicts, and maintaining engagement. Keeping up with changing labor regulations adds further difficulty.

How AI Simplifies HR Tasks

AI can automate resume analysis, create unbiased interview questions, draft training materials, and monitor employee sentiment. Tools like ChatGPT, Gemini, and Perplexity AI help HR professionals make quicker, data-driven decisions, streamline communication, and improve workplace fairness.

Crafting Effective Prompts for HR Tasks

This section offers practical, role-specific prompts to help HR managers leverage AI tools like ChatGPT, Gemini, and Perplexity AI for hiring, employee engagement, training, and performance management. Each prompt includes a realistic scenario, an optimized prompt, and a clear explanation of how it works, empowering HR professionals to enhance efficiency, ensure fairness, and make data-driven decisions across key human resources functions.

1. Screening Candidate Resumes

Scenario

An HR manager needs to identify the most qualified candidates from 50 resumes for a marketing manager role.

> **Prompt**
> *"You are a senior HR manager. Analyze the attached resumes and shortlist the top five candidates who meet these requirements: minimum five years' marketing experience, leadership in campaigns, proficiency in data analytics, and excellent communication skills."*

How It Works

Using a tool like ChatGPT, Gemini, or Perplexity AI, first upload resumes in a format like .pdf or .docx. Next, enter the prompt specifying candidate criteria and submit. The AI evaluates each resume, ranks candidates, and generates a concise shortlist with rationale to streamline hiring decisions.

2. Drafting a Job Description

Scenario

An HR manager needs to draft a comprehensive job description for a new role that will attract qualified candidates and clearly define the responsibilities and qualifications.

Prompt

"You are a talent acquisition specialist. Draft a clear and compelling job description for a [specify job title, e.g., 'Senior Software Engineer'] at a [company type, e.g., fast-growing tech startup]. Include sections for key responsibilities, required qualifications, preferred skills, and a brief company overview to attract top talent."

How It Works

Using a tool like ChatGPT or Gemini, first enter the prompt, ensuring you specify the job title and company type. Next, submit. The AI will generate a structured job description that can be customized and posted on job boards.

3. Preparing for Candidate Interviews

Scenario

An HR manager or hiring manager needs to prepare a structured set of interview questions for a specific job opening to ensure a fair and consistent evaluation of all shortlisted candidates.

Prompt

"You are a recruitment consultant. Draft a comprehensive interview question guide for a [specify job title, e.g., 'Senior Product Manager']. The guide should include 10 questions covering a mix of behavioral, situational, and technical skills. For each question, provide a brief explanation of what to look for in an ideal answer."

How It Works

Using a tool like ChatGPT or Gemini, first enter the prompt, ensuring you specify the job title. Next, submit. The AI will generate a structured interview guide that helps you conduct more effective and objective interviews.

4. Drafting Personalized Onboarding Plans

Scenario

An HR manager needs to create tailored onboarding plans for new hires in different departments.

Prompt

"You are an HR onboarding specialist. Draft individualized onboarding plans for three new hires in sales, product development, and HR operations. Each plan should outline a 30-day schedule including training modules, key meetings, and performance milestones tailored to their roles."

How It Works

Using a tool like ChatGPT, Perplexity AI, or Gemini, first enter the prompt, ensuring you specify the new hire's role. Next, submit. The AI will generate a structured and actionable onboarding plan that you can adapt and share with the new employee and their manager.

5. Creating Employee Conflict Resolution Plans

Scenario

An HR manager needs to resolve a workplace dispute between two team members over task responsibilities.

Prompt

"You are an experienced HR conflict resolution specialist. Using the attached incident reports and employee statements, draft a resolution plan including an objective summary, mediation steps, responsibilities, and follow-up actions to rebuild trust and teamwork."

How It Works

Using a tool like ChatGPT, Gemini, or Perplexity AI, first upload incident documents in a format like .pdf or .docx. Next, enter the prompt and submit. The AI synthesizes details, identifies key issues, and produces a structured, actionable plan enabling professional conflict resolution.

6. Designing Personalized Training Plans

Scenario

An HR manager needs to create customized training plans for mid-level managers promoted to leadership roles.

> **Prompt**
>
> *"You are an experienced HR training coordinator. Using the attached profiles, draft individualized 60-day training plans for three newly promoted mid-level managers, addressing leadership, conflict resolution, and strategic planning with clear milestones and recommended resources."*

How It Works

Using a tool like ChatGPT, Gemini, or Perplexity AI, first upload manager profiles or performance summaries in a format like .pdf or .docx. Next, enter the prompt and submit. The AI identifies skill gaps and generates tailored training plans to boost leadership readiness and managerial success.

Lawyers

The Essential Role of a Lawyer

Lawyers play a vital role in society by advising clients, representing them in disputes, and ensuring compliance with laws and regulations. Their work spans legal research, drafting contracts, negotiating settlements, and advocating in court. Effective lawyers protect client interests, uphold justice, and provide strategic guidance across civil, criminal, corporate, and specialized legal fields.

Common Challenges Faced by Lawyers

Lawyers often grapple with time-consuming document reviews, researching case law under tight deadlines, managing complex client communications, and keeping up with evolving legal precedents. Balancing workload with accuracy remains a key challenge.

How AI Simplifies Legal Tasks

AI tools like ChatGPT, Gemini, and Perplexity AI can automate contract analysis, streamline legal research, draft correspondence, and summarize lengthy documents, freeing lawyers to focus on strategy and client advocacy.

Crafting Effective Prompts for Legal Tasks

This section provides targeted prompts to help lawyers harness AI tools like ChatGPT, Gemini, and Perplexity AI in tasks such as contract review, legal research, drafting motions, and client communication. Each prompt includes a realistic scenario, an optimized prompt, and a clear explanation of how it works, enabling legal professionals to save time, improve accuracy, and deliver more effective counsel across diverse areas of practice.

1. Summarizing Complex Contracts

Scenario

A lawyer wants to quickly understand the key terms and potential risks in a 40-page commercial lease agreement.

Prompt

"You are a corporate lawyer. Summarize the attached commercial lease agreement in 300 words, highlighting critical clauses, tenant and landlord obligations, renewal terms, and any identified risks."

How It Works

Using a tool like ChatGPT or Gemini, first upload the contract in PDF or Word format. Next, enter the prompt and submit. The AI will extract essential contract details and generate a concise summary to facilitate faster comprehension and client advisement.

2. Drafting Demand Letters

Scenario

A lawyer needs to write a formal demand letter for unpaid invoices on behalf of a corporate client.

Prompt

"You are an experienced commercial litigation attorney. Using the provided contract details, draft a clear, assertive demand letter requesting payment of outstanding invoices totaling [insert amount]. Reference relevant contract terms, specify a payment deadline, and outline potential legal actions for continued nonpayment."

How It Works

Using a tool like ChatGPT or Gemini, first enter the prompt. Next, specify the amount involved, with contract details or correspondence summaries directly below it. Then, submit. The AI produces a polished demand letter with precise legal language to support effective debt recovery.

3. Conducting Case Law Research

Scenario

A lawyer preparing for trial needs a quick overview of recent rulings on non-compete agreements.

Prompt

"You are a legal research specialist. Provide a summary of the most recent case law on the enforceability of non-compete clauses in [insert jurisdiction], including key precedents, relevant statutes, and trends over the past five years."

How It Works

Using a tool like Perplexity AI or Gemini, first enter the prompt, explicitly specifying the relevant jurisdiction. Next, submit. The AI will scan authoritative legal databases and return a concise, up-to-date summary to aid in trial preparation.

4. Creating Customized NDAs

Scenario

A lawyer needs a non-disclosure agreement (NDA) tailored to a technology partnership involving sensitive intellectual property.

Prompt

"You are a corporate attorney. Using provided project details, draft a tailored non-disclosure agreement for a partnership between a software developer and hardware manufacturer. Include clauses on confidentiality scope, permitted disclosures, duration, governing law, and breach remedies."

How It Works

Using a tool like ChatGPT, Perplexity AI, or Gemini, first enter the prompt. Next, provide project specifics such as parties, purpose, and confidential information type directly below the prompt. Then, submit. The AI will generate a precise, legally compliant NDA draft protecting both parties' interests.

5. Motion to Dismiss International Trade Dispute

Scenario

A Ghanaian lawyer's client is being sued by a foreign company. The lawyer argues that the Ghanaian court does not have the authority to hear the case because the original contract requires all disputes to be settled through arbitration in Singapore.

Prompt

"You are a Ghanaian commercial lawyer. Using the attached contract and statement of claim, draft a motion to dismiss for lack of jurisdiction. Cite the arbitration clause under Ghana's Alternative Dispute Resolution Act and relevant case law."

How It Works

Using a tool like ChatGPT, Perplexity AI, or Gemini, first upload the contract and statement of claim in PDF or Word format. Next, enter the prompt and submit. The AI will draft a jurisdiction-based motion aligned with Ghanaian procedural law.

6. Preparing Deposition Questions in a Serious Fraud Case

Scenario

A lawyer representing a financial institution suspects that a senior manager has embezzled funds and needs a detailed deposition outline to uncover their role.

> **Prompt**
>
> *"You are a white-collar crime attorney. Using the attached fraud investigation report and financial statements, draft 25 deposition questions covering fund transfers, suspicious transactions, falsified records, and potential co-conspirators."*

How It Works

Using a tool like ChatGPT or Gemini, first upload relevant investigation reports and financial documents in PDF or Word format. Next, enter the prompt and submit. The AI reviews evidence and generates a logically structured deposition outline to aid the examination of key fraud issues.

Linguists

Essential Role of a Linguist

Linguists analyze language structure, meaning, and usage, working in academia, translation, technology, and cultural preservation. They design grammars, document endangered languages, develop language-learning tools, and support fields like computational linguistics and speech recognition.

Common Challenges Faced by Linguists

Linguists struggle with synthesizing large corpora, accurately documenting endangered languages, aligning translations with cultural nuances, and performing time-consuming comparative analyses across multiple languages or dialects.

How AI Simplifies Linguistics Tasks

AI tools like ChatGPT, Gemini, and Perplexity AI assist linguists by automating text analysis, generating cross-lingual summaries, identifying semantic patterns, and suggesting culturally appropriate translations. They streamline corpus compilation, accelerate linguistic annotation, and support endangered language revitalization by quickly processing vast textual datasets.

Crafting Effective Prompts for Linguistics Tasks

This section provides practical, role-specific prompts that show how linguists can leverage large language models (LLMs) like ChatGPT, Gemini, and Perplexity AI to enhance linguistic research and analysis. Each prompt includes a realistic scenario, an optimized prompt, and an explanation of how the AI generates precise outputs.

1. Compiling Dialectal Variations

Scenario

A linguist is documenting regional variations of a language and needs examples of different vocabulary, idioms, and pronunciations.

> **Prompt**
>
> *You are a field linguist. Compile a list of 30 regional words, idiomatic expressions, and pronunciation differences for [language name], specifying the dialect and region for each entry.*

How It Works

Using a tool like ChatGPT, Gemini, or Perplexity AI, first enter the prompt, specifying the language name. Next, submit. The AI will generate a detailed, structured table of dialectal variations for sociolinguistic research or language preservation.

2. Analyzing Morphosyntactic Structures

Scenario

A linguist is researching how grammatical structures differ between related languages for a comparative linguistics paper.

Prompt

You are a comparative linguist. Generate a detailed table comparing noun phrase structures, verb conjugation patterns, and word order in [Language A] and [Language B]. Include example sentences and brief explanations of key differences.

How It Works

Using a tool like ChatGPT, Gemini, or Perplexity AI, first enter the prompt, specifying both languages. Next, submit. The AI will produce a comprehensive comparative table highlighting grammatical contrasts to aid typological studies.

3. Documenting Endangered Language Vocabulary

Scenario

A linguist is compiling a dictionary for an endangered language and requires categorized vocabulary lists.

Prompt

"You are an endangered language specialist. Using the provided text samples or recordings, generate a categorized vocabulary list of at least 100 words for [endangered language], grouped by themes such as food, family, environment, and traditional practices, with English translations."

How It Works

Using a tool like ChatGPT, Gemini, or Perplexity AI, first enter the prompt, specifying the language. Next, upload text or transcriptions (e.g., in .txt or .mp3 format) and submit. The AI will extract and organize bilingual vocabulary lists, facilitating dictionary compilation and revitalization efforts.

4. Creating Phonetic Transcription Guides

Scenario

A linguist needs an accurate phonetic transcription guide to illustrate pronunciation differences for students.

Prompt

"You are a phonologist. Generate an International Phonetic Alphabet (IPA) transcription guide for [language or dialect], including examples of common words and a brief description of unique phonemes or tonal features."

How It Works

Using a tool like ChatGPT, Gemini, or Perplexity AI, first enter the prompt, specifying the language or dialect. Next, submit. The AI will deliver a clear IPA guide with sample words and explanations to support language teaching.

5. Designing Sociolinguistic Surveys

Scenario

A linguist planning fieldwork on language attitudes wants a detailed survey to collect community perspectives.

> **Prompt**
>
> *"You are a sociolinguist. Draft a 25-question survey for speakers of [language or dialect] covering dialect preferences, code-switching situations, perceived status of local varieties, and attitudes toward standard forms. Use a mix of multiple-choice, Likert scale, and open-ended questions."*

How It Works

Using a tool like ChatGPT, Gemini, or Perplexity AI, first enter the prompt, specifying the language and community context. Next, submit. The AI will generate a professionally structured survey instrument to facilitate community language attitude research.

6. Comparing Politeness Strategies Across Languages

Scenario

A sociolinguist analyzing intercultural communication needs examples of how politeness is expressed differently.

Prompt

"You are a sociolinguist. Generate examples of greetings, requests, refusals, and apologies in [Language A] and [Language B], with brief explanations of how each reflects cultural norms regarding politeness and hierarchy."

How It Works

Using a tool like ChatGPT, Gemini, or Perplexity AI, first enter the prompt, specifying both languages. Next, submit. The AI will provide side-by-side examples with cultural commentary, aiding intercultural communication and teaching.

Marketer

Essential Role of a Marketer

Marketers develop strategies to promote products, build brand awareness, engage audiences, and drive conversions. They research markets, craft messaging, create content, manage campaigns, and analyze performance data to optimize outcomes.

Common Challenges Faced by Marketers

Marketers often struggle to keep up with content demands across channels, personalize messaging at scale, interpret complex analytics, and maintain consistent branding. Time constraints and rapid market changes add further pressure.

How AI Simplifies Marketing Tasks

AI tools such as ChatGPT, Gemini, Perplexity AI, Invideo AI, and Canva AI help marketers automate content creation, generate personalized copy, A/B test headlines, analyze customer sentiment, and design visuals. These capabilities streamline workflows, improve targeting, and empower marketers to launch more effective, data-driven campaigns while freeing time for creative strategy.

Crafting Effective Prompts for Marketing Tasks

This section presents practical, role-specific prompts to help marketers and advertising professionals leverage large language models (LLMs) like ChatGPT, Gemini, Perplexity AI, and specialized tools like Canva AI and Invideo AI for daily tasks. These examples are grounded in real-world marketing challenges, from drafting compelling ad copy and creating social media strategies to generating engaging video content and advanced image editing for campaigns.

1. Integrated Script-to-Video Generation

Scenario

A marketer needs a complete teaser video for a product launch using prompt chaining on a single platform.

> **Prompt**
> *"Draft a 30-second teaser script for [product/event], highlighting unique features, emotional appeal, and a compelling call-to-action. Based on the script, generate a dynamic 30-second video, including energetic background music, branded text overlays, and fast-paced transitions for Instagram Reels and TikTok."*

How It Works

Using a tool like Invideo AI or Canva AI, with integrated video generation, first enter the prompt, specifying your product or event details. Next, submit. The AI will first create the script and then, using its video generation capabilities, produce a polished, professional marketing video efficiently.

2. Crafting Compelling Ad Copy

Scenario

A digital marketer needs to write concise and engaging ad copy for a new product launch across various platforms, ensuring it resonates with the target audience.

> **Prompt**
>
> *"You are a seasoned copywriter. Draft three distinct ad copy variations for a new [specify product type, e.g., eco-friendly reusable coffee cup] targeting [specify target audience, e.g., environmentally conscious young urban professionals]. Each variation should be optimized for a different platform: Instagram (short & visual), Facebook (engaging & descriptive), and Google Ads (keyword-focused). Include a strong Call-to-Action for each."*

How It Works

Using a tool like ChatGPT, Gemini, or Microsoft Copilot, first enter the prompt. Next, specify the product type and target audience within the prompt entry, and submit. The AI will generate tailored ad copy to effectively reach different segments of your target audience on multiple platforms.

3. Developing a Social Media Content Calendar

Scenario

A social media manager needs to plan a month's worth of content for a new brand, ensuring a consistent posting schedule and diverse content types.

Prompt

"You are a social media strategist. Develop a one-month content calendar for [brand name, e.g., 'Aura Skincare'] targeting [target audience, e.g., women aged 25-45 interested in natural beauty]. Include daily post ideas, recommended platforms, content formats, and key hashtags for each post."

How It Works

Using a tool like ChatGPT, Perplexity AI, or Gemini, first enter the prompt. Next, specify the brand name and target audience within the prompt entry, and submit. The AI will create a structured content plan, complete with themes, formats, and hashtags, to streamline your social media efforts.

4. Product Image Editing for a Marketing Campaign

Scenario

A digital marketer needs to adapt a single product photograph into several different visual assets for a social media campaign. They need to change the background, maintain the product's look, and add new elements seamlessly.

Prompt

"You are a professional digital artist. Based on the attached product image, change the background to a sunny, outdoor cafe scene. Ensure the product's texture and lighting remain consistent with its original appearance."

How It Works

Using a tool like ChatGPT, Gemini (*Nano Banana)*, or Canva AI, first, enter the prompt. Next, upload the image in a format like .jpeg or .png. Then, submit. The AI will provide the first-pass edit.

Follow-up Prompt

Once the first edit is complete, you can provide follow-up prompts to continue refining the image. The AI will remember the original image and all previous edits. For example, you can now enter: "*Now, add a second version of the same image. Change the cafe scene background to a vibrant city street at night and add a rainy effect.*"

5. Creating a Product Explainer Video Script

Scenario

A marketing team needs an engaging script for a short product explainer video (60-90 seconds) to highlight key features and benefits for potential customers.

Prompt

"You are a video content strategist. Draft a 60-90 second explainer video script for [insert product name, e.g., 'EcoCharge Portable Solar Charger']. Focus on key features, benefits, and a strong problem-solution narrative. Include visual cues for each scene, a compelling voice-over script, and a clear Call-to-Action."

How It Works

Using a tool like ChatGPT, Gemini, or Canva AI, first enter the prompt, specifying the product name in the prompt entry. Next, submit. The AI will generate a detailed video script, complete with scene descriptions and voice-over text, ready for production.

6. Revitalizing an Underperforming Ad Campaign

Scenario

A marketing team's ad campaign for a new product isn't achieving expected engagement or conversions.

> **Prompt**
>
> *"You are a digital marketing consultant. Analyze the provided ad copy or video script below for [e.g., Skincare Product Campaign]. Evaluate messaging, visuals, and targeting strategy. Provide specific recommendations to improve engagement and conversions, including revised copy, alternative scripts, creative ideas, and improved audience segmentation."*

How It Works

Using a tool like ChatGPT or Gemini, first enter the prompt, specifying your product campaign within the prompt entry. Next, provide your ad text or video script below it and submit. The AI will critique and optimize messaging and creative elements for stronger ROI across campaign formats.

Mechanical Engineer

Essential Role of a Mechanical Engineer

Mechanical engineers design, analyze, and oversee the production of mechanical systems such as engines, HVAC systems, and manufacturing equipment. They perform calculations, select materials, create technical drawings, and ensure that systems meet performance, safety, and regulatory standards.

Common Challenges Faced by Mechanical Engineers

Mechanical engineers often face difficulties managing complex design iterations under tight deadlines, integrating feedback across teams, maintaining accuracy in extensive calculations, and staying updated with evolving engineering standards. Additionally, preparing detailed documentation for compliance and stakeholder communication can be time-consuming.

How AI Simplifies Mechanical Engineering Tasks

AI tools like ChatGPT, Gemini, and Perplexity AI assist mechanical engineers by automating repetitive calculations, generating technical documentation, drafting design reports, offering quick clarifications on standards, and creating compelling visual design prototypes.

Crafting Effective Prompts for Mechanical Engineering Tasks

This section provides actionable, role-specific prompts demonstrating how mechanical engineers can leverage large language models (LLMs) like ChatGPT, Gemini, and specialized AI tools such as Leonardo AI, to streamline their workflows. From drafting detailed technical reports to generating conceptual design visuals, each prompt includes a realistic scenario, an optimized instruction, and a clear explanation of how AI delivers precise outputs.

1. Summarizing Technical Test Data

Scenario

An engineer needs a concise summary of a thermal performance test report for a new HVAC component.

> **Prompt**
>
> *"You are a mechanical engineer. Summarize the key findings, anomalies, and recommended actions from the attached thermal performance test report."*

How It Works

Using a tool like ChatGPT or Gemini, first upload the report in a format like .pdf or .docx. Next, enter the prompt and submit. The AI will analyze data tables, charts, and text, producing a clear summary highlighting critical results and actionable design or performance recommendations.

2. Optimizing Gearbox Design Calculations

Scenario

A mechanical engineer is finalizing a gearbox for an industrial machine and needs precise calculations for optimal gear ratios, torque distribution, and bearing selection.

Prompt

"You are a mechanical engineer. Given the provided design requirements and load conditions, calculate optimal gear ratios, torque values, and suggest appropriate bearings. Provide detailed step-by-step calculations and recommendations to minimize vibration and maximize lifespan."

How It Works

Using a tool like ChatGPT or Gemini, first enter the prompt. Next, paste the design specifications in a table or text format directly below it. Then, submit. The AI will process engineering parameters, generating precise calculations and design insights to streamline mechanical validation.

3. Creating a Conceptual 3D Design Prototype

Scenario

A mechanical engineer needs a quick visual prototype of a compact hydraulic pump for a design review meeting.

> ***Prompt***
>
> *"Generate a photorealistic 3D render of a compact hydraulic pump (200x150x150 mm) with inlet/outlet ports, an integrated pressure gauge, and ergonomic mounting brackets suitable for stakeholder presentations."*

How It Works

Using a tool like Midjourney or Leonardo AI, first enter the prompt and submit. The AI will produce a high-quality visual prototype to communicate design intent effectively during early-stage reviews.

4. Drafting Maintenance Procedures for Mechanical Systems

Scenario

A mechanical engineer needs to create step-by-step maintenance guidelines for a mechanical system to train technicians.

Prompt

"You are a mechanical engineer. Draft detailed maintenance guidelines for a [e.g., horizontal centrifugal pump], covering routine inspections, lubrication schedules, common wear points, and troubleshooting tips for vibration, seal leaks, and reduced flow."

How It Works

Using a tool like ChatGPT or Gemini, first enter the prompt with equipment details. Next, submit. The AI organizes clear, actionable procedures aligned with industry best practices to support technician training and enhance reliability.

5. Evaluating Finite Element Analysis (FEA) Results

Scenario

An engineer has completed FEA simulations on a load-bearing bracket but needs a clear interpretation of stress distribution and potential failure points.

Prompt

"You are a mechanical engineer. Interpret the attached FEA report for a load-bearing bracket. Highlight maximum stress regions, safety factors, potential failure points, and recommend design modifications to improve strength or reduce weight."

How It Works

Using a tool like ChatGPT or Gemini, first upload the FEA report in a format like .pdf or .docx. Next, enter the prompt and submit. The AI reviews simulation data and images, delivering an accessible interpretation with actionable design suggestions.

6. Automating Compliance Document Drafting

Scenario

A mechanical engineer needs to prepare a compliance document for a new machine to meet ISO 12100 safety standards.

Prompt

"You are a mechanical engineer. Draft a compliance report for the attached machine design per ISO 12100:2010 standards. Detail identified hazards, safety measures, and residual risks using formal technical language suitable for regulatory submission."

How It Works

Using a tool like ChatGPT, Perplexity AI, or Gemini, first upload the design description or drawings in .pdf or .docx format. Next, enter the prompt and submit. The AI generates a professional compliance document referencing relevant standards to optimize regulatory workflows.

Medical Doctor

Essential Role of a Medical Doctor

Medical doctors diagnose, treat, and manage illnesses while guiding patients on preventive care. They interpret complex data, create treatment plans, and work with healthcare teams to improve patient outcomes.

Common Challenges Faced by Medical Doctors

Doctors face time constraints, extensive documentation, and the need to stay current with rapidly evolving medical knowledge. Interpreting lab results, imaging, and patient histories can overwhelm even experienced clinicians.

How AI Simplifies Medical Tasks

AI tools like ChatGPT, Gemini, and Perplexity AI help doctors by summarizing research, generating patient-friendly explanations, drafting documentation, and supporting differential diagnoses. These tools reduce administrative burdens, improve accuracy, and free up time for compassionate, patient-centered care, empowering doctors to deliver more efficient, informed, and personalized healthcare.

Crafting Effective Prompts for Medical Tasks

This section presents practical prompts showing doctors how to use AI tools like ChatGPT, Gemini, and Perplexity AI to improve efficiency in tasks like research summarization, patient communication, and clinical documentation. Each prompt includes a realistic scenario, a precise command, and an explanation of how AI-generated outputs enhance patient care and streamline medical workflows.

1. Summarizing Complex Research Papers

Scenario

A doctor needs to quickly understand a dense 30-page cardiology study before a patient consultation.

> **Prompt**
>
> *"You are a medical researcher. Summarize the attached 30-page cardiology research paper in 500 words. Highlight study objectives, key findings, limitations, and clinical implications, maintaining medical accuracy and clarity."*

How It Works

Using a tool like ChatGPT or Gemini, first upload the research paper in a format like .pdf or .docx. Next, enter the prompt and submit. The AI will condense the detailed study into a concise, clear summary to support evidence-based consultations.

2. Explaining Complex Lab Results to Patients

Scenario

A physician receives comprehensive lab panels with abnormal values and wants to explain them clearly to the patient.

Prompt

"You are an internal medicine physician. Translate the attached lab results, including abnormal liver enzymes and electrolytes, into clear, patient-friendly explanations. Describe what each abnormal value means, possible causes, and recommended next steps in language accessible to non-medical patients."

How It Works

Using a tool like ChatGPT, Perplexity AI, or Gemini, first upload the lab report in .pdf or image format. Next, enter the prompt and submit. The AI uses OCR to read the data and produces easy-to-understand explanations that facilitate patient communication.

3. Generating Differential Diagnosis Lists

Scenario

A doctor sees a patient with nonspecific symptoms like fatigue, weight loss, and night sweats, and needs a structured list of possible diagnoses.

> **Prompt**
>
> *"You are an experienced diagnostician. Given symptoms of fatigue, unexplained weight loss, and night sweats, generate a prioritized differential diagnosis list. Include common and serious conditions, recommended initial tests, and brief rationales for each possibility."*

How It Works

Using a tool like ChatGPT or Perplexity AI, first enter the prompt with the patient's symptoms. Next, submit. The AI will produce a structured, ranked list of possible diagnoses with suggested investigations, aiding diagnostic reasoning.

4. Creating Informed Consent Summaries

Scenario

A surgeon needs to provide a clear, understandable consent summary for a complex orthopedic procedure.

Prompt

You are a medical writer. Draft a patient-friendly informed consent summary for [e.g., total knee replacement surgery], explaining the procedure, risks, benefits, alternatives, and postoperative care in plain language suitable for patients with no medical background."

How It Works

Using a tool like ChatGPT, Gemini, or Perplexity AI, first enter the prompt, specifying the procedure details. Next, submit. The AI translates complex medical information into accessible consent material, facilitating ethical patient decision-making.

5. Managing Patients with Multiple Chronic Diseases

Scenario

A physician is treating a patient with hypertension, type 2 diabetes, and chronic kidney disease and needs a coordinated management plan.

> **Prompt**
>
> *"You are a primary care physician. Draft an integrated care plan for a patient with hypertension, Type 2 diabetes, and stage 3 chronic kidney disease. Include medication adjustments, dietary and lifestyle guidance, and specialist referrals in patient-friendly language."*

How It Works

Using a tool like ChatGPT, Perplexity AI, or Gemini, first enter the prompt with patient conditions. Next, submit. The AI synthesizes guidelines into a comprehensive, understandable management plan, promoting coordinated care.

6. Designing a Home Monitoring Protocol

Scenario

A doctor wants a plan for home monitoring of blood pressure, glucose, and weight for a heart failure patient.

Prompt

"You are a cardiologist. Develop a step-by-step home monitoring protocol for daily blood pressure, glucose, and weight tracking, including thresholds for concern and when to contact the clinic, presented in clear, patient-friendly language."

How It Works

Using a tool like ChatGPT or Perplexity AI, first enter the prompt with patient-specific details. Next, submit. The AI generates a tailored monitoring plan, empowering patients to detect early warning signs and engage with their healthcare team proactively.

Musician

Essential Role of a Musician

Musicians create, perform, arrange, and record music for diverse audiences and platforms. They compose original pieces, reinterpret existing works, and collaborate with other creatives to produce compelling musical content. Their contributions are essential in entertainment, education, cultural preservation, and emotional storytelling.

Common Challenges Faced by Musicians

Musicians often face challenges such as creative block, time-consuming composition processes, limited access to studio resources, and the complexity of music production tools. Additionally, independent artists may struggle with branding, marketing, and producing industry-level demos.

How AI Simplifies Musical Tasks

AI tools like Suno, ChatGPT, and Canva AI assist musicians with melody generation, lyric writing, arrangement ideas, and even producing fully synthesized audio. These tools help speed up music creation, overcome creative block, and enhance the quality of outputs—empowering musicians to focus on their artistic vision.

Crafting Effective Prompts for Musical Tasks

This section explores how musicians can strategically use AI tools like Suno, ChatGPT, Perplexity, Microsoft Copilot and Canva AI to streamline songwriting, arrangement, and creative production workflows. Each prompt includes a realistic scenario, a carefully constructed prompt, and a "How it works" explanation that outlines the tools' role in generating melodies, writing lyrics, or preparing professional-grade assets.

1. Generating Original Song Lyrics

Scenario

A singer-songwriter is experiencing creative block and needs emotionally resonant lyrics for a ballad about healing from heartbreak.

Prompt

You are a professional songwriter. Write emotionally expressive lyrics for a ballad titled "After the Storm," focusing on themes of heartbreak, inner strength, and emotional healing. Structure the lyrics with verses, a chorus, and a bridge.

How It Works

Using a tool like ChatGPT, Microsoft Copilot, or Perplexity AI, first enter the prompt. Next, submit. The AI will generate well-structured, emotionally resonant lyrics, providing a strong creative foundation for the songwriter to build upon.

2. Designing a Promotional Poster for a Music Release

Scenario

A musician is preparing to release a new jazz EP and wants a sleek promotional poster for social media.

> **Prompt**
>
> *"Design a promotional poster for the release of a jazz EP titled 'Midnight Groove.' Include abstract saxophone art, dark blue and gold tones, the release date (July 21), and a QR code placeholder for streaming platforms."*

How It Works

Using a tool like ChatGPT, Gemini, or Perplexity AI, first enter the prompt. Next, submit. The AI will suggest creative text and design ideas, which you can further refine and develop into a professional poster using graphic tools like Canva AI.

3. Genre-Blending Song Creation

Scenario

A songwriter wants to experiment by blending Afrobeats with Lo-fi elements for a niche streaming audience.

Prompt

"You are a songwriter creating a 90-second demo combining Afrobeats rhythms and percussion with Lo-fi textures and ambient melodies. The theme is 'sunrise on a quiet street in Accra.' Include vocals with subtle storytelling elements."

How It Works

Using a tool like Suno or Microsoft Copilot, first enter the prompt. Next, submit. The AI will generate a hybrid sound composition layering rhythmic and melodic elements, allowing experimentation with cross-genre production.

4. Refining a Gospel Song for Clarity and Impact

Scenario

A gospel musician has drafted a heartfelt worship song but feels the lyrics need refinement.

Prompt

"You are a gospel songwriter. Refine the provided worship song lyrics to improve lyrical flow, emotional resonance, and scriptural depth, while preserving the original voice and message. Ensure a consistent structure including verse, chorus, and bridge, with a reverent and uplifting tone."

How It Works

Using a tool like ChatGPT, Microsoft Copilot, or Perplexity AI, first enter the prompt. Next, paste your draft lyrics directly below it and submit. The AI will enhance structure, imagery, and word choice, delivering polished lyrics that maintain your spiritual intent.

5. Designing a Music Promotion Campaign

Scenario

An independent gospel artist is preparing to release a new single and wants a structured marketing plan to promote it across social media, email, and streaming platforms.

> **Prompt**
>
> *"You are a digital music marketer. Develop a comprehensive 2-week promotional campaign for a gospel single release. Include daily content ideas, platform-specific strategies (Instagram, TikTok, YouTube Shorts), a pre-save link plan, fan engagement tactics, and email marketing tips. Tailor the campaign to an independent artist working with a modest budget."*

How It Works

Using a tool like ChatGPT, Gemini, or Canva AI, first enter the prompt. Next, submit. The AI will create a detailed plan with platform-focused actions and engagement templates to drive organic growth within budget constraints.

6. Preparing for Media Interviews on a New Music Release

Scenario

A rising artist is about to appear on radio and television to promote their debut single and needs to prepare for interviews.

Prompt

"You are a professional music publicist coaching a new artist for their first radio and TV interviews about their debut single. Develop a 2-minute personal narrative, key talking points, anticipated questions with sample responses, and tips for confident delivery, tone, posture, and adapting to different interview formats."

How It Works

Using a tool like ChatGPT or Gemini, first enter the prompt. Next, submit. The AI will generate a complete media coaching brief to help the artist effectively communicate their story and engage audiences professionally.

Nutritionist

Essential Role of a Nutritionist

Nutritionists assess dietary needs, develop personalized meal plans, and provide evidence-based guidance to promote health and manage conditions like diabetes, obesity, or hypertension. They translate nutritional science into actionable strategies tailored to individual or population needs.

Common Challenges Faced by Nutritionists

They often deal with time-consuming client documentation, complex dietary restrictions, and the challenge of translating lab data into clear nutritional recommendations. Staying updated on evolving research while keeping clients motivated adds further strain.

How AI Simplifies Nutrition Tasks

AI tools like ChatGPT, Gemini, and Perplexity AI streamline repetitive tasks, automate personalized meal plans, and summarize clinical research. They assist in interpreting nutritional data, generating education materials, and tailoring advice—allowing nutritionists to focus more on behavior coaching and outcome tracking.

Crafting Effective Prompts for Nutrition Tasks

This section presents practical prompts tailored for nutritionists to enhance client care, research, and content creation. Using tools like ChatGPT, Gemini, and Perplexity AI, nutrition professionals can streamline dietary planning, analyze clinical data, translate research into action, and generate personalized educational resources.

1. Creating a Personalized Meal Plan

Scenario

A nutritionist needs to develop a 7-day meal plan for a new client with Type 2 diabetes who also follows a vegetarian diet.

> **Prompt**
>
> *"You are a licensed nutritionist. Develop a 7-day vegetarian meal plan for an adult with Type 2 diabetes. Each day should include three balanced meals and snacks, with proper macronutrient distribution to maintain stable blood sugar levels."*

How It Works

Using a tool like ChatGPT or Gemini, first enter the prompt. Next, submit. The AI will generate a structured, day-by-day meal plan tailored for glycemic control and vegetarian preferences, including nutritional breakdowns and portion guidance.

2. Analyzing Nutritional Deficiencies from a Food Diary

Scenario

A client submits a 5-day food diary to their nutritionist, who needs to identify potential micronutrient deficiencies.

> ***Prompt***
>
> *"You are a registered dietitian. Analyze the 5-day food diary provided below and identify likely vitamin or mineral deficiencies. Recommend specific dietary adjustments or food sources to address these gaps, considering the client's age (45), gender (female), and moderately active lifestyle."*

How It Works

Using a tool like ChatGPT or Perplexity AI, first enter the prompt. Next, paste the food diary as plain text directly below it and submit. The AI will evaluate dietary patterns, identify common nutrient deficiencies, and suggest nutrient-rich foods to support evidence-based nutritional guidance.

3. Creating a Culturally Sensitive Meal Plan for Diabetic Clients

Scenario

A nutritionist is working with a newly diagnosed Type 2 diabetic client from Ghana who wants to manage their condition without giving up traditional meals.

Prompt

"You are a licensed nutritionist. Create a 7-day culturally appropriate meal plan for a Ghanaian client newly diagnosed with Type 2 diabetes. Incorporate traditional dishes like waakye, fufu, banku, and kontomire while focusing on blood sugar management. Include portion recommendations, meal timing, and healthy substitutes."

How It Works

Using a tool like ChatGPT or Gemini, first enter the prompt. Next, submit. The AI will produce a balanced meal plan that fits diabetic needs and local cuisine, suggesting ingredient modifications to maintain cultural relevance and glycemic control.

4. Analyzing Patient Nutrient Deficiencies from Lab Results

Scenario

A nutritionist receives lab test results for a client showing low levels of iron, vitamin D, and B12, and needs to quickly create a targeted dietary intervention plan.

> ***Prompt***
>
> *"You are a clinical nutritionist. Analyze the following lab values for a patient and recommend dietary strategies to address deficiencies in iron, vitamin D, and vitamin B12. Include food sources, serving sizes, and meal timing recommendations for optimal absorption."*
>
> ***lab values example:***
>
> *Serum iron: 35 µg/dL*
> *Vitamin D: 18 ng/mL*
> *Vitamin B12: 180 pg/mL*

How It Works

Using a tool like ChatGPT or Gemini, first enter the prompt. Next, paste the lab values as text directly below it and submit. The AI will generate an evidence-based nutritional intervention plan with food recommendations and practical meal planning tips.

5. Translating Research into Client-Friendly Education

Scenario

A nutritionist reads a complex 30-page research paper on the gut-brain axis and wants to translate the findings into a simplified handout for clients with IBS.

> ***Prompt***
>
> *"You are a registered nutritionist. Summarize the key findings of the attached research paper on the gut-brain axis in simple, client-friendly language. Structure the output as an educational handout for individuals managing Irritable Bowel Syndrome (IBS), including practical lifestyle and dietary takeaways."*

How It Works

Using a tool like ChatGPT, Perplexity, or Gemini, first upload the research document in PDF or Word format. Next, enter the prompt and submit. The AI will extract key findings and translate them into an accessible, empathetic client resource for dietary and lifestyle support.

6. Personalized Dietary Plan for Multiple Conditions

Scenario

A clinical nutritionist needs a comprehensive dietary plan for a 58-year-old client with a gastric ulcer, Type 2 diabetes, and stage 1 hypertension.

> ***Prompt***
>
> *"You are a clinical nutritionist. Create a 7-day culturally adaptable meal plan for a 58-year-old client with gastric ulcer, Type 2 diabetes, and stage 1 hypertension. The client is from [e.g., Ethiopia] and prefers traditional dishes. Avoid ulcer triggers, maintain low glycemic index meals, limit sodium intake, and suggest food substitutions where necessary. Include a daily rationale for main meals."*

How It Works

Using a tool like ChatGPT or Perplexity AI, first enter the prompt with the client's cultural background. Next, submit. The AI will generate an integrative meal plan aligning with the client's multiple dietary needs and cultural preferences.

Pharmacist

Essential Role of a Pharmacist

Pharmacists ensure the safe and effective use of medications by dispensing prescriptions, advising on dosage, identifying drug interactions, and counseling patients. They serve as a critical bridge between prescribers and patients in the healthcare system.

Common Challenges Faced by Pharmacists

Pharmacists often face time constraints, complex drug regimens, frequent updates in pharmacology, and challenges in patient adherence. Managing high prescription volumes while ensuring accuracy and patient understanding adds to their workload.

How AI Simplifies Pharmacy Tasks

AI tools like ChatGPT, Gemini, and Perplexity AI help pharmacists streamline patient counseling, check drug interactions, summarize treatment protocols, and create educational materials. This enhances clinical accuracy, improves patient communication, and supports informed, efficient decision-making in both retail and clinical settings.

Crafting Effective Prompts for Pharmacy Tasks

This section presents practical AI prompts tailored for pharmacists, helping them optimize core responsibilities like medication counseling, interaction checking, and clinical communication. Using large language models (LLMs) such as ChatGPT, Gemini, and Perplexity AI, pharmacists can enhance efficiency, accuracy, and patient safety in daily workflows. Each prompt features a realistic scenario, a strategically designed prompt, and a brief explanation of how the AI's response supports pharmaceutical decision-making.

1. Counseling on New Medication Use

Scenario

A pharmacist needs to explain metformin to a newly diagnosed type 2 diabetes patient.

> ***Prompt***
>
> *You are a clinical pharmacist. Explain to a newly diagnosed type 2 diabetes patient how metformin works, how to take it safely, and possible side effects. Use clear, non-technical language suitable for patient understanding.*

How It Works

Using a tool like ChatGPT, Perplexity AI, or Gemini, first enter the prompt. Next, submit. The AI will generate a concise, patient-friendly explanation that enhances understanding and supports safe medication use.

2. Detecting Potential Drug Interactions

Scenario

A pharmacist is reviewing a patient's medication list and wants to check for possible interactions between prescribed drugs and recent over-the-counter supplements.

Prompt

"You are a clinical pharmacist. Review a patient's list of prescribed medications and recent over-the-counter supplements provided below. Identify potential drug-drug or drug-supplement interactions and explain their clinical significance in concise terms."

How It Works

Using a tool like ChatGPT or Gemini, first enter the prompt. Next, paste the complete list of medications and supplements as text directly below it and submit. The AI will analyze interaction risks and provide clinical explanations to support therapy adjustments or patient counseling.

3. Generating Patient-Friendly Drug Guides

Scenario

A pharmacist needs to provide a simplified drug information leaflet to a patient starting a new prescription.

> ***Prompt***
>
> *"You are a drug information pharmacist. Generate a patient-friendly drug guide for [insert drug name], including its purpose, dosage instructions, common side effects, storage advice, and safety tips. Use simple language appropriate for a non-medical audience."*

How It Works

Using a tool like ChatGPT, Perplexity AI, or Gemini, first enter the prompt with the medication name. Next, submit. The AI will deliver an easy-to-understand, pharmacist-grade guide suitable for patients with limited medical knowledge.

4. Supporting Geriatric Polypharmacy Management

Scenario

A pharmacist is managing a senior patient with multiple chronic conditions taking over ten medications. They must assess for safety and adherence.

Prompt

"You are a professional pharmacist. Review the following geriatric patient's medication list. Identify polypharmacy concerns such as therapeutic duplication, inappropriate dosing, high-risk interactions, or administration challenges. Recommend a simplified regimen aligned with geriatric pharmacotherapy best practices."

How It Works

Using a tool like ChatGPT or Perplexity AI, first enter the prompt. Next, paste the complete medication list as text directly below it and submit. The AI will identify risks and suggest optimization strategies for safer, more manageable therapy.

5. Oncology Medication Verification and Side Effect Profiling

Scenario

A hospital pharmacist must verify a complex chemotherapy order for a breast cancer patient. They also need to counsel the patient about expected side effects.

.

Prompt

"You are an oncology pharmacist. Review the following chemotherapy regimen for a breast cancer patient. Verify dosing, check for drug interactions, and summarize expected side effects, monitoring requirements, and key counseling points."

How It Works

Using a tool like ChatGPT or Gemini, first enter the prompt. Next, upload or paste the chemotherapy plan as PDF or text with relevant lab results, and submit. The AI will cross-check dosing standards, highlight contraindications, and generate an accessible patient education summary.

6. Remote Counseling via Telepharmacy

Scenario

A rural pharmacist providing telepharmacy services needs to offer a concise medication counseling session for a newly discharged heart failure patient.

> ***Prompt***
>
> *"You are a clinical pharmacist providing telepharmacy services. Prepare a simplified, patient-friendly explanation of carvedilol, lisinopril, and furosemide for a newly discharged heart failure patient, covering drug purpose, administration timing, side effects, and warning signs."*

How It Works

Using a tool like ChatGPT or perplexity AI, first enter the prompt. Next, submit. The AI will create a clear, comprehensive guide designed for virtual counseling, supporting effective patient understanding without in-person contact.

Project Manager

Essential Role of a Project Manager

Project managers plan, execute, and oversee projects to ensure timely delivery, within scope and budget. They coordinate teams, manage resources, mitigate risks, and maintain communication among stakeholders. Their leadership is critical to aligning project goals with organizational objectives.

Common Challenges Faced by Project Managers

Project managers often navigate scope creep, shifting priorities, resource constraints, and interdepartmental communication gaps. Maintaining timelines, managing stakeholder expectations, and ensuring team alignment, while adapting to unexpected changes, are constant hurdles.

How AI Simplifies Project Management Tasks

AI platforms like Microsoft Copilot, ChatGPT, and Gemini help streamline scheduling, draft status reports, and provide risk assessments. They assist with data analysis, automate routine communications, and improve decision-making through predictive insights, freeing managers to focus on strategic leadership.

Crafting Effective Prompts for Project Management Tasks

This section presents AI prompts tailored to essential project management responsibilities. Each scenario reflects real-world use cases, optimized for ChatGPT, perplexity, Gemini, and Microsoft Copilot. Mastering these prompts enables project managers to enhance productivity, improve stakeholder communication, and manage complex tasks with greater confidence and efficiency.

1. Writing a Project Status Update for Executives

Scenario

A project manager is required to deliver a weekly status update to the executive team on an ongoing project.

> ***Prompt***
>
> *"You are a project manager preparing a concise weekly status report for senior executives on the following project. Draft an update highlighting current progress, key risks or blockers, and planned next steps. Use professional, non-technical language suitable for an executive audience."*

How It Works

Using a tool like ChatGPT or Gemini, first enter the prompt. Next, paste the project summary and update notes as plain text directly below it and submit. The AI will format the information into a polished, executive-level status report.

2. Evaluating Project Management Methodologies

Scenario

A project manager needs a structured comparison of Agile, Waterfall, and Hybrid methodologies for a product development project.

Prompt

"You are a project management strategist. Compare Agile, Waterfall, and Hybrid methodologies for the project described below. Address suitability, flexibility, stakeholder engagement, risk management, delivery cadence, and documentation practices."

How It Works

Using a tool like ChatGPT or Gemini, first enter the prompt. Next, paste or upload the project context in .pdf or .docx format. Then, submit. The AI will provide a structured comparison highlighting strengths, weaknesses, and use-case suitability for each methodology.

3. Generating a Stakeholder Communication Plan

Scenario

A project manager needs to develop a communication plan for a cross-functional product launch involving internal departments and external vendors.

> ***Prompt***
>
> *"You are a project manager. Based on the project described below, generate a stakeholder communication plan that includes key stakeholder groups, communication objectives, preferred channels, frequency of communication, and responsibility assignments."*

How It Works

Using a tool like ChatGPT, Gemini, or Microsoft Copilot, first enter the prompt. Next, paste the project and stakeholder details as plain text directly below it. Then, submit. The AI will generate a detailed communication plan that aligns messaging strategies with stakeholder roles and influence levels.

4. Risk Identification and Categorization

Scenario

During the initiation phase of a construction project, the project manager must identify potential risks across technical, financial, legal, and environmental domains.

> ***Prompt***
>
> *"You are a project risk consultant identifying potential risks in the initiation phase of a construction project. Based on the project information provided, categorize risks as technical, financial, legal, or environmental and provide brief rationales for each."*

How It Works

Using a tool like ChatGPT, Gemini, or Perplexity AI, first enter the prompt. Next, paste the project information as plain text directly below it, and submit. The AI will analyze and organize key risks with justifications to support early mitigation planning.

5. Project Budget Estimation with Historical Data

Scenario

A project manager is tasked with estimating the budget for a new project by leveraging historical cost data from similar projects.

> ***Prompt***
>
> *"You are a project estimation expert. Using provided historical cost data and relevant new project details (e.g., scope, duration, complexity), generate a budget estimate. Include assumptions, cost category breakdowns, and adjustments for scale and inflation."*

How It Works

Using a tool like ChatGPT, Gemini, or Microsoft Copilot, first enter the prompt. Next, paste the historical data and project specifications as text directly below it, and submit. The AI will produce an accurate, structured budget estimate to aid transparent planning and reduce the risk of over- or underestimation.

6. Procurement Strategy Design

Scenario

A project manager is planning a complex initiative involving multiple vendors and needs a tailored procurement strategy.

Prompt

"You are a procurement strategist. Based on the project details below, design a comprehensive procurement strategy. Include contract types, vendor selection criteria, risk mitigation measures, and timeline alignment."

How It Works

Using a tool like ChatGPT, Perplexity, or Gemini, first enter the prompt. Next, paste the project description, procurement needs, and timeline constraints as plain text directly below it, and submit. The AI will recommend a comprehensive sourcing strategy that enhances vendor engagement and control over procurement risks.

Research Scientist

Essential Role of a Research Scientist

Research scientists investigate complex problems, develop hypotheses, design experiments, and analyze data to advance knowledge across fields such as biology, physics, chemistry, and technology. Their work fuels scientific innovation, informs policy, and supports technological and medical breakthroughs.

Common Challenges Faced by Research Scientists

Scientists often struggle with time-consuming literature reviews, synthesizing vast data, refining methodologies, and drafting publication-ready documents. Juggling grant writing, data visualization, and keeping pace with emerging findings adds further strain.

How AI Simplifies Research Tasks

AI tools like ChatGPT, Perplexity AI, and Gemini support research scientists by streamlining literature synthesis, summarizing dense scientific articles, generating citations, proposing experimental designs, debugging code, and visualizing complex data. These tools enable researchers to accelerate discovery while maintaining precision and scholarly integrity.

Crafting Effective Prompts for Research Tasks

This section presents targeted prompts to help research scientists harness the capabilities of AI tools such as ChatGPT, Gemini, and Perplexity AI. From experimental design and data interpretation to literature review and academic writing, these prompts are designed to accelerate workflows, improve clarity, and support rigorous scientific inquiry.

1. Drafting a Research Problem Statement

Scenario

A research scientist needs a concise problem statement for a proposal on nanomaterial-based drug delivery.

> ***Prompt***
>
> *You are a biomedical researcher preparing a grant proposal. Compose a concise, 150-word problem statement focused on nanomaterials for targeted cancer drug delivery. Emphasize clinical relevance, current research gaps, and the study's significance. Use formal academic language suitable for submission to funding bodies.*

How It Works

Using a tool like ChatGPT or Gemini, first enter the prompt. Next, submit. The AI will generate a clear, structured, and academically sound problem statement defining the research gap, scope, and justification suitable for grant applications or publication introductions.

2. Designing a Literature Review Outline

Scenario

A research scientist is preparing a comprehensive literature review on climate-resilient crop genetics and wants a structured outline.

Prompt

"You are an agricultural research scientist preparing a literature review on climate-resilient crop varieties. Create a detailed outline that includes major themes such as genetic adaptation, biotechnology, drought tolerance, pest resistance, and future research directions. Organize sections logically and use bullet points for subtopics. Limit scope to research published from 2019 to 2024."

How It Works

Using a tool like ChatGPT or Perplexity AI, first enter the prompt. Next, submit. The AI will produce a coherent, thematically organized outline reflecting recent research trends, providing a structured writing blueprint.

3. Drafting a Grant Proposal Abstract

Scenario

A scientist needs to craft a compelling abstract that highlights the significance, methodology, and potential impact of their project on antibiotic resistance.

Prompt

"You are a biomedical research scientist writing a grant proposal abstract of about 350 words. Focus on a study of novel antimicrobial peptides targeting antibiotic-resistant bacteria. Describe the research gap, hypothesis, methods, and expected public health impact. Use formal, persuasive language tailored for grant reviewers."

How It Works

Using a tool like ChatGPT or Gemini, first enter the prompt. Next, submit. The AI outputs a concise, well-structured abstract highlighting originality, objectives, methodology, and potential outcomes, ready for grant submission.

4. Identifying Gaps in Literature for Novel Research

Scenario

A research scientist in neuroscience is developing a proposal and needs help identifying under-explored areas in recent literature.

Prompt

"You are a neuroscience researcher analyzing literature from the past five years on cognitive decline in aging. Identify under-explored or conflicting areas based on recent studies. Cite key references where relevant. Summarize research gaps clearly to support novel study proposals."

How It Works

Using a tool like Perplexity AI or Gemini, first enter the prompt. Next, submit. The AI synthesizes recent scholarly literature, flagging overlooked topics and unresolved questions to help refine research focus.

5. Designing a Mixed-Methods Research Framework

Scenario

A health science researcher is planning a mixed-methods study to explore the relationship between workplace stress and cardiovascular health.

Prompt

"You are a research methodologist designing a mixed-methods study on occupational stress and cardiovascular health in nurses. Outline research questions, qualitative and quantitative data collection strategies, sequencing (e.g., explanatory design), and data integration methods such as triangulation."

How It Works

Using a tool like ChatGPT or Gemini, first enter the prompt. Next, submit. The AI will generate a structured framework with stepwise methodology guidance suitable for protocol development or ethics application.

6. Designing a Pilot Study for Banana Flour Processing

Scenario

A research scientist at a food innovation lab is developing a proposal for turning overripe bananas into high-value flour.

Prompt

"You are a food process engineer. Draft a pilot study outline to compare three drying methods (solar, convection, and freeze-drying) in producing banana flour from overripe plantains. Include objectives, methodology, sample size, analysis parameters (e.g., moisture, texture, microbial load), and potential challenges."

How It Works

Using a tool like ChatGPT, Perplexity AI, or Gemini, first enter the prompt. Next, submit. The AI will produce a detailed pilot study design covering sampling and data analysis, ideal for grant proposals or feasibility research.

Soccer Coach

Essential Role of a Soccer Coach

A soccer coach guides individual players and entire teams toward peak performance through tactical training, physical conditioning, and motivational leadership. Coaches develop game strategies, assess opponents, and make real-time decisions during matches to optimize outcomes.

Common Challenges Faced by Soccer Coaches

Soccer coaches often struggle with creating personalized training regimens, analyzing opponent strategies, balancing team dynamics, and scouting emerging talent. Time constraints and limited access to advanced analytics also hinder strategic planning.

How AI Simplifies Soccer Coaching Tasks

AI tools such as ChatGPT, Gemini, and Perplexity AI streamline scouting reports, generate game plans, analyze match statistics, and suggest training drills tailored to player needs. These platforms can evaluate player performance trends and simulate opponent tactics, enabling coaches to make data-informed decisions that enhance team cohesion and competitive edge.

Crafting Effective Prompts for Soccer Coaching Tasks

This section presents targeted prompts designed to assist soccer coaches in optimizing tactical planning, player development, and match preparation using tools like ChatGPT, Gemini, and Perplexity AI. Each prompt includes a real-world coaching scenario, a precision-crafted prompt, and a clear explanation of how the AI processes user input to generate actionable insights that align with team and performance objectives.

1. Designing a Weekly Training Schedule

Scenario

A soccer coach wants to structure a balanced weekly training schedule for a U-17 team focused on fitness, technical skills, and match tactics.

> ***Prompt***
>
> *You are a youth soccer coach. Create a detailed 5-day training schedule for a U-17 team focusing on fitness, ball control, positional drills, and tactical scrimmages. Ensure the plan balances physical conditioning and technical skills, tailored to the age and skill level of the players.*

How It Works

Using a tool like ChatGPT, Perplexity AI, or Gemini, first enter the prompt. Next, submit. The AI will generate a day-by-day training plan structured to optimize fitness, technical development, and tactical understanding.

2. Tactical Breakdown from Match Footage

Scenario

A soccer coach wants to evaluate their team's defensive structure during a recent match to identify weaknesses in transition after losing possession.

> **Prompt**
>
> *Act as a professional football tactical analyst. Analyze the attached 10-minute match video focusing on defensive transitions during the first half. Our team wears blue jerseys and started on the left side of the pitch. Evaluate defensive shape, player spacing, and recovery after turnovers, then recommend tactical improvements.*

How It Works

Using a tool like ChatGPT Plus/Pro, or Gemini Pro, first enter the prompt. Next, upload the match footage in a format like .mp4. Then, submit. The AI provides a professional tactical report highlighting defensive strengths, weaknesses, and suggested strategies.

3. Pre-Match Strategy Development

Scenario

A soccer coach is preparing for an upcoming match against a team known for high pressing and rapid wing play.

Prompt

"Act as a seasoned football strategist. Draft a pre-match tactical plan to counter an opponent known for high pressing and rapid wing play. Our team excels at midfield control and long-ball transitions. Suggest formations, in-possession and out-of-possession tactics, and key player roles to exploit weaknesses in the opponent's press."

How It Works

Using a tool like ChatGPT, Perplexity AI, or Gemini, first enter the prompt. Next, submit. The AI will produce a comprehensive game plan tailored to your team's strengths and the opposition's playing style.

4. Post-Match Performance Analysis

Scenario

A soccer coach wants to critically analyze their team's performance based on key tactical objectives to guide the next week's training focus.

Prompt

"You are a professional football performance analyst. Based on the attached match video, evaluate our team's performance on possession control, transition speed, and defensive organization. Highlight strengths, weaknesses, and recommend three key training focus areas. Our team wears red and white jerseys and started on the right side of the pitch."

How It Works

Using a tool like ChatGPT Plus/Pro, or Gemini Pro, first enter the prompt. Next, upload the video in a format like .mp4. Then, submit. The AI generates a concise evaluation report with actionable insights to guide future training sessions.

5. Designing a Position-Specific Training Plan

Scenario

A soccer coach wants to create a focused training routine for central midfielders to improve spatial awareness, passing under pressure, and defensive positioning.

Prompt

"You are a UEFA-certified football coach. Design a detailed 5-day training plan specifically for central midfielders to improve spatial awareness, quick passing under pressure, and defensive positioning against high-pressing teams. Include drill names, session duration, and objectives."

How It Works

Using a tool like ChatGPT or Perplexity AI, first enter the prompt. Next, submit. The AI will create a targeted training schedule to improve tactical and technical proficiency at a critical position.

6. Designing Position-Specific Drills

Scenario

A soccer coach is preparing a midweek training session focused on improving winger performance.

> **Prompt**
>
> *"You are an elite football development coach. Design a 90-minute winger-focused training session that improves acceleration, crossing accuracy under pressure, and decision-making in the final third. Include drill names, duration, required equipment, and coaching points."*

How It Works

Using a tool like ChatGPT or Perplexity AI, first enter the prompt. Next, submit. The AI will generate a structured session plan with warm-ups, technical drills, cooldowns, and coaching tips designed to maximize winger performance.

Software Engineer

Essential Role of a Software Engineer

Software engineers design, develop, test, and maintain software systems that power applications, websites, embedded systems, and enterprise tools. They translate technical specifications into functional code, solve complex problems, optimize performance, and ensure scalability and security. Their work forms the digital infrastructure for businesses, governments, and global platforms.

Common Challenges Faced by Software Engineers

Software engineers often face tight deadlines, debugging bottlenecks, integration complexities, and ambiguous feature requests. Managing large codebases, ensuring cross-platform compatibility, and writing efficient, maintainable code require significant time and focus.

How AI Simplifies Software Engineering Tasks

AI tools like ChatGPT, Canva AI, Gemini, Microsoft Copilot, and Perplexity AI assist software engineers by generating boilerplate code, debugging, suggesting architecture patterns, optimizing queries, translating pseudocode into code, and reviewing logic. These tools accelerate development workflows, reduce cognitive load, and improve productivity across the software lifecycle.

Crafting Effective Prompts for Software Engineering Tasks

This section presents strategic prompts tailored for software engineers seeking to accelerate development, troubleshoot issues, and streamline project workflows using tools like ChatGPT, Gemini, Canva AI, and Microsoft Copilot. Whether you are prototyping, optimizing algorithms, documenting APIs, or reviewing code, each prompt features a realistic scenario, an optimized prompt, and a clearly explained outcome to demonstrate how AI can enhance modern software engineering tasks with efficiency and precision.

1. Debugging an Authentication Error

Scenario

A software engineer encounters a persistent login failure in a web app's authentication flow.

> ***Prompt***
>
> *"You are a senior software engineer. Analyze this authentication error log and identify the root cause. Suggest a fix and best practices to prevent similar issues."*

How It Works

Using a tool like ChatGPT or Gemini, first enter the prompt. Next, paste the error log as plain text (.txt) directly below it, and submit. The AI will diagnose the issue and propose actionable solutions.

2. Refactoring Legacy Code for Performance

Scenario

A software engineer is tasked with optimizing a legacy codebase that is slowing down application performance.

> ***Prompt***
>
> *"You are a software engineer. Refactor the legacy code provided below to improve performance, readability, and maintainability. Include inline comments to explain your changes and suggest further architectural improvements if applicable."*

How It Works

Using a tool like ChatGPT, Microsoft Copilot, or Gemini, first enter the prompt. Next, paste the legacy code snippet from a text-based file (.txt, .py, .js) directly below it, and submit. The AI will analyze inefficiencies, refactor the code for improved readability, performance, and maintainability, and include inline comments explaining the changes.

3. Generating API Documentation

Scenario

A software engineer needs to quickly generate clear documentation for a new RESTful API.

Prompt

"You are a software engineer. Generate complete and developer-friendly API documentation for the following endpoints, including request/response examples, parameters, error codes, and authentication requirements."

How It Works

Using a tool like ChatGPT, Perplexity AI, or Gemini, first enter the prompt. Next, paste the relevant API code or route definitions from a text-based file (.txt, .js, .py) directly below it, and submit. The AI will generate complete, developer-friendly API documentation suitable for developer portals or onboarding.

4. Debugging Complex Code Logic

Scenario

A software engineer encounters a persistent logical error in a backend service handling dynamic pricing algorithms.

> ***Prompt***
>
> *"You are a senior backend developer. Analyze the following Python function for logic errors affecting dynamic price calculation and suggest precise fixes with a brief explanation."*

How It Works

Using a tool like ChatGPT, Microsoft Copilot, or Gemini, first enter the prompt. Next, paste the problematic code from a text-based file (.txt, .py) directly below it, and submit. The AI will analyze the logic, identify edge cases or faulty conditions, and recommend corrected code with clear inline commentary.

5. Reviewing Algorithm Efficiency

Scenario

A software engineer is optimizing a Python algorithm that performs data filtering on large datasets. They want an analysis of its time and space complexity.

> ***Prompt***
>
> *"You are a senior software engineer. Review the following Python algorithm for time and space complexity. Identify any inefficiencies and propose optimization strategies without changing the algorithm's core logic."*

How It Works

Using a tool like ChatGPT or Gemini, first enter the prompt. Next, paste the full Python algorithm from a Python file (.py) directly below it, and submit. The AI will evaluate the algorithm's time and space complexity, identify inefficiencies, and propose optimization strategies that preserve the core logic.

6. Designing RESTful API Endpoints

Scenario

A backend software engineer is tasked with developing a RESTful API for a bookstore management system.

> ***Prompt***
>
> *"You are a backend engineer. Design RESTful API endpoints for a bookstore system that allows listing all books, retrieving book details by ID, updating inventory levels, and managing customer orders. Ensure proper use of HTTP methods and endpoint structure."*

How It Works

Using a tool like ChatGPT, Canva AI, or Gemini, first enter the prompt. Next, submit. The AI will create a set of well-structured RESTful API endpoints, recommending URI paths, HTTP methods (GET, POST, PUT, DELETE), and concise descriptions of functionality.

System Analyst

Essential Role of a System Analyst

System analysts assess business needs and translate them into clear technical specifications. They evaluate current systems, model workflows, and recommend improvements aligned with organizational goals. Acting as intermediaries between stakeholders and developers, they ensure solutions are feasible, efficient, and aligned with requirements.

Common Challenges Faced by System Analysts

System analysts face unclear requirements, legacy system constraints, and shifting priorities. Balancing stakeholder expectations with technical feasibility, ensuring compliance, and maintaining traceable documentation are persistent challenges, especially in fast-evolving environments.

How AI Simplifies System Analysis Tasks

AI tools like ChatGPT, Perplexity AI, and Gemini assist in clarifying requirements, drafting documentation, and modeling processes. They streamline analysis, reduce ambiguity, and support faster, more informed decision-making.

Crafting Effective Prompts for System Analysis Tasks

This section presents professionally aligned prompts tailored to key responsibilities in system analysis. Each prompt reflects a real-world task and is optimized for platforms like ChatGPT, Perplexity AI, Gemini, or Microsoft Copilot. By learning how to craft these prompts, analysts can improve the quality, speed, and clarity of their outputs while reducing manual effort and misinterpretation in early system design phases.

1. Clarifying Ambiguous Requirements

Scenario

A system analyst receives vague and conflicting requirements for a CRM enhancement. To proceed with design, they must refine the statements into clear, testable specifications.

> **Prompt**
> *"You are a system analyst. Rewrite the following requirements to be specific, testable, and implementation-ready. Identify missing or inconsistent information."*

How It Works

Using a tool like ChatGPT or Gemini, first enter the prompt. Next, paste the requirements from a text-based file (.docx, .txt) directly below it and submit. The AI analyzes and rewrites the input, producing precise, structured requirements.

2. Designing a Process Flow Diagram

Scenario

A system analyst is tasked with mapping out the process for handling customer complaints. They want to generate a structured flow diagram for stakeholder review and technical implementation.

> ***Prompt***
>
> *"You are a system analyst. Based on the process description provided below, generate a structured process flow with decision points, actors, and process steps. Present the output in a format suitable for BPMN tools or flowchart editors."*

How It Works

Using a tool like ChatGPT, Perplexity AI, or Microsoft Copilot, first enter the prompt. Next, paste the process description from a text-based file (.txt, .docx) directly below it and submit. The AI will generate a structured process flow with decision points, actors, and steps, formatted suitably for BPMN tools or flowchart editors.

3. Comparing System Integration Options

Scenario

A system analyst is evaluating whether to integrate an HR system with an external payroll provider via REST API or file-based batch processing.

Prompt

"You are a systems integration consultant. Compare REST API integration versus file-based batch processing for the use case described below. Include pros and cons, data synchronization frequency, reliability, scalability, and maintainability considerations."

How It Works

Using a tool like ChatGPT or Gemini, first enter the prompt. Next, paste the system integration context from a text-based file (.txt, .docx) directly below it and submit. The AI will produce a comparative analysis covering pros and cons, data synchronization frequency, reliability, scalability, and maintainability, supporting informed decision-making.

4. Writing a System Requirements Specification (SRS)

Scenario

A system analyst is tasked with drafting a System Requirements Specification for a new inventory management module.

> ***Prompt***
>
> *"You are a system analyst. Create a structured System Requirements Specification (SRS) based on the project description below. Include sections for functional and non-functional requirements, user roles, system interfaces, and constraints."*

How It Works

Using a tool like ChatGPT or Microsoft Copilot, first enter the prompt. Next, paste the project background or feature list from a text-based file (.txt, .docx) directly below it and submit. The AI will generate a structured SRS draft containing functional and non-functional requirements, user roles, system interfaces, and constraints.

5. Simulating User Scenarios for System Testing

Scenario

A system analyst needs to validate the completeness of requirements for a banking app's loan application module by simulating a range of realistic user scenarios.

> ***Prompt***
>
> *You are a system analyst. Based on the functional requirements provided below, generate realistic user scenarios and edge cases to test the completeness of a loan application module in a banking app."*

How It Works

Using a tool like ChatGPT or Perplexity AI, first enter the prompt. Next, paste the functional requirements from a text-based file (.txt, .docx) directly below it and submit. The AI will create realistic user scenarios and edge cases to validate requirement completeness and uncover gaps, supporting early design validation and system testing readiness.

6. Evaluating Feasibility of System Upgrade

Scenario

A system analyst is reviewing whether to upgrade a legacy ERP system to a modern cloud-based solution.

> ***Prompt***
>
> *"You are a system analyst. Based on the ERP system description provided below, evaluate the feasibility of upgrading to a cloud-based solution. Consider technical compatibility, data migration, cost, scalability, and operational impact."*

How It Works

Using a tool like ChatGPT, Gemini, or Microsoft Copilot, first enter the prompt. Next, paste the ERP system description or specifications from a text-based file (.txt, .docx) directly below it and submit. The AI will produce a structured feasibility analysis addressing technical compatibility, data migration, cost, scalability, and operational impact to guide upgrade planning and stakeholder decisions.

Teacher

Essential Role of a Teacher

Teachers design and deliver curriculum-aligned instruction, assess learner progress, and adapt pedagogy to accommodate varying abilities and learning styles. They cultivate intellectual curiosity, critical thinking, and social development, serving as foundational figures in students' academic and personal growth.

Common Challenges Faced by Teachers

Teachers face time constraints, large class sizes, administrative burdens, and the need to differentiate instruction for diverse learners. Maintaining engagement, designing inclusive content, managing assessments, and staying current with evolving standards further compound their workload.

How AI Simplifies Teaching Tasks

AI platforms such as ChatGPT, Perplexity AI, Gemini, and Microsoft Copilot support teachers by generating lesson plans, quizzes, grading rubrics, and personalized activities. These tools help reduce repetitive tasks, accelerate content creation, and enhance instructional design—enabling teachers to focus more on interactive and student-centered learning experiences.

Crafting Effective Prompts for Teaching Tasks

This section presents structured prompts tailored to core teaching responsibilities. Each prompt addresses real classroom tasks—lesson planning, assessment design, feedback, and differentiated instruction—optimized for platforms like ChatGPT, Gemini, Perplexity AI, and Microsoft Copilot to support pedagogical effectiveness.

1. Hands-On Math Lesson Planning

Scenario

An elementary school teacher needs to design a dynamic and interactive math lesson on a challenging concept like fractions, using engaging methods to ensure young students grasp the topic.

> **Prompt**
> *"You are an elementary math teacher in an urban school. Design a hands-on math lesson on fractions for a 3rd-grade class, using visual aids and real-world examples to make the concepts accessible and fun. The lesson should include interactive games, manipulatives, and problem-solving exercises that reinforce the understanding of fractions and their applications."*

How It Works

Using a tool like ChatGPT, Microsoft Copilot, or Gemini, first enter the prompt. Next, submit. The AI will generate a structured lesson plan complete with activity ideas and real-world examples to make fractions easier to teach and learn.

2. Interactive Activities for Special Education

Scenario

A special education teacher needs a collection of interactive, accessible activities to reinforce core language arts skills for students with learning disabilities.

Prompt

"Assume the role of a special education teacher working with a group of 4th-grade students with learning disabilities. Create a set of 10 interactive activities that can be used during a language arts lesson to reinforce vocabulary, reading comprehension, and writing skills in an engaging and accessible manner."

How It Works

Using a tool like ChatGPT or Gemini, first enter the prompt. Next, submit. The AI will provide a list of tailored activities that can be immediately implemented in the classroom to support the students' learning needs.

3. Creating Differentiated Practice Exercises

Scenario

A teacher needs differentiated reading tasks for Grade 5 students at varying ability levels.

Prompt

"You are a professional 5th grade English teacher in an urban public school. Using the learning objective provided below, create three differentiated English practice activities; one each for advanced, intermediate, and emerging readers. For each activity, include a short nonfiction passage, clear instructions, response tasks, and the correct answers."

How It Works

Using a tool like ChatGPT or Perplexity AI, first enter the prompt. Next, paste the learning objective from a text-based file (.txt, .docx) directly below it, then submit. The AI will generate leveled practice activities, each with corresponding nonfiction passages, instructions, and answer keys.

4. Generating Formative Quiz Questions

Scenario

A teacher wants to assess students' understanding of a Grade 8 science topic—photosynthesis—through a quick formative quiz.

> ***Prompt***
>
> *"You are a professional science teacher. Based on the topic of photosynthesis and the Grade 8 science standard provided below, generate a 10-question formative quiz. Include a mix of multiple-choice, short-answer, and true/false items. Provide the correct answers after each question."*

How It Works

Using a tool like ChatGPT or Perplexity AI, first enter the prompt. Next, paste the relevant standard from a text-based file (.txt, .docx) directly below it, then submit. The AI will create a 10-question formative quiz aligned with the standard, featuring a mix of question types and an answer key.

5. Writing Personalized Student Feedback

Scenario

A teacher has reviewed a set of student essays and wants to generate constructive, individualized feedback for each student.

Prompt

"You are a professional teacher. Based on the student's essay excerpt and rubric score provided below, write personalized feedback highlighting one strength, one area for improvement, and a final encouraging remark. Keep the tone constructive and student-friendly."

How It Works

First, If the essay is in hardcopy, convert it into a text-based format (.txt or .docx) using a scanning app such as Google Lens or any OCR tool. Next, open your AI tool of choice, such as ChatGPT, Gemini, or Microsoft Copilot.Enter the prompt, then paste the student's essay excerpt and corresponding rubric score directly below it and submit. The AI will generate personalized, constructive feedback that highlights strengths, identifies areas for improvement, and concludes with a supportive, encouraging remark suitable for students.

6. Designing a Conceptual Quiz on Newton's Laws

Scenario

A physics teacher is introducing Newton's Laws and needs a short quiz to check students' conceptual understanding.

Prompt

"You are a professional physics teacher. Create a 10-question conceptual quiz on Newton's three laws of motion for high school students. Use a mix of multiple-choice and short-answer questions. Provide an answer key."

How It Works

Using a tool like ChatGPT or Perplexity AI, first enter the prompt. Next, submit. The AI will generate a 10-question conceptual quiz on Newton's three laws of motion for high school students, with a mix of multiple-choice and short-answer formats, and correct answers.

Technical Writer

Essential Role of a Technical Writer

Technical writers transform complex technical information into clear, accessible documentation. They create manuals, user guides, API references, and instructional content that support end users, developers, and stakeholders. Their writing ensures that products and systems can be understood, used, and maintained efficiently.

Common Challenges Faced by Technical Writers

Technical writers often face challenges such as incomplete technical input, tight deadlines, rapidly changing specifications, and the need to balance clarity with technical accuracy. Maintaining consistency across documentation formats and ensuring content aligns with both user needs and product updates can be demanding.

How AI Simplifies Technical Writing Tasks

AI tools like ChatGPT, Perplexity, Microsoft Copilot, and Gemini assist technical writers by generating structured drafts, rewriting complex content for clarity, maintaining style consistency, summarizing technical notes, and suggesting formatting improvements. These tools accelerate documentation workflows, reduce editing time, and support scalable, user-friendly content production.

Crafting Effective Prompts for Technical Writing Tasks

This section presents professionally aligned prompts tailored to the key responsibilities of technical writers. Each prompt reflects real-world documentation tasks and is optimized for AI tools like ChatGPT, Perplexity AI, Gemini, or Microsoft Copilot. They help writers produce accurate, accessible, and user-centered content efficiently across technical and product documentation workflows.

1. Drafting a User Guide Section

Scenario

A technical writer needs to draft a user guide section for a new software feature that is part of a larger product launch.

> ***Prompt***
>
> *"You are a technical writer. Based on the feature description provided below, draft a clear, user-friendly guide section. Include step-by-step instructions, use cases, and expected outputs."*

How It Works

Using a tool like ChatGPT, Perplexity AI, or Gemini, first enter the prompt. Next, paste the feature description from a text-based file (.txt, .docx) directly below it and submit. The AI will generate a well-structured, task-oriented section ready for documentation.

2. Converting Technical Notes into Formal Documentation

Scenario

A technical writer receives fragmented engineering notes from a developer describing a new API function. The writer must convert these into formal, standardized documentation suitable for publication.

> ***Prompt***
>
> *"You are a technical writer. Convert the technical notes provided below into formal API documentation. Include function purpose, parameters, return types, usage examples, and formatting aligned with documentation standards."*

How It Works

Using a tool like ChatGPT, Gemini, or Microsoft Copilot, first enter the prompt. Next, paste the raw technical notes and specifications from a text-based file (.txt, .docx) directly below it and submit. The AI will transform the notes into formal, standardized API documentation.

3. Writing Patient Information Leaflets for a Pharmaceutical Product

Scenario

A technical writer is assigned to draft a patient information leaflet for an over-the-counter medication, ensuring clarity, regulatory compliance, and accessibility for non-expert readers.

> ***Prompt***
>
> *"You are a technical writer. Based on the product information provided, write a patient information leaflet (PIL) for a pharmaceutical product. Include sections on usage, dosage, precautions, side effects, and storage. Ensure the tone is accessible to the general public."*

How It Works

Using a tool like ChatGPT or Gemini, first enter the prompt. Next, paste the product data sheet or formulation details from a text-based file (.txt, .pdf) directly below it and submit. The AI will produce a clear, easy-to-understand patient information leaflet that is compliant with health literacy and regulatory requirements.

4. Drafting Operating Instructions for a Medical Device

Scenario

A technical writer wants to produce clear operating instructions for a portable ECG monitoring device used by healthcare professionals in outpatient settings.

> ***Prompt***
>
> *"You are a technical writer. Using the device specifications provided below, draft operating instructions for a portable ECG machine. Include setup steps, usage procedures, safety notes, and indications for troubleshooting."*

How It Works

Using a tool like ChatGPT, Perplexity AI, or Gemini, first enter the prompt. Next, paste the device specifications from a text-based file (.txt, .docx) directly below it and submit. The AI will create professional, clinical-grade operating instructions covering setup, usage, safety precautions, and troubleshooting guidance.

5. Creating a Troubleshooting Guide for a Vehicle Infotainment System

Scenario

A technical writer is documenting a troubleshooting section for a car's infotainment system manual, aimed at non-technical vehicle owners.

Prompt

"You are a technical writer. Based on the issues listed below, write a troubleshooting section for a vehicle infotainment system. Include problem symptoms, likely causes, and clear user-level solutions."

How It Works

Using a tool like ChatGPT, Perplexity AI, or Gemini, first enter the prompt. Next, paste a list of common issues and system notes from a text-based file (.txt, .docx) directly below it and submit. The AI will generate a structured troubleshooting section in user-friendly language.

6. Writing Assembly Instructions for a Home Appliance

Scenario

A technical writer is tasked with creating step-by-step assembly instructions for a consumer appliance, such as an air purifier or standing fan.

> ***Prompt***
>
> *"You are a technical writer. Using the mechanical specifications and part list provided below, write step-by-step assembly instructions for this home appliance. Use clear, numbered steps and reference labeled parts."*

How It Works

Using a tool like ChatGPT or Gemini, first enter the prompt. Next, paste the part list and manufacturer notes from a text-based file (.txt, .docx) directly below it and submit. The AI will produce clear, stepwise assembly instructions.

Technician

Essential Role of a Technician

Technicians who maintain and repair electrical and electronic gadgets play a crucial role in ensuring the functionality, safety, and longevity of a wide range of devices, from household appliances to industrial equipment. Their work involves diagnosing faults, repairing or replacing components, running system checks, and documenting repair actions to maintain performance and compliance standards.

Common Challenges Faced by Technicians

Technicians often encounter challenges such as identifying obscure faults, interpreting incomplete service histories, sourcing compatible replacement parts, and keeping up with evolving technologies, and time constraints in urgent repair scenarios.

How AI Simplifies Technician work

Generative AI tools streamline fault diagnosis, repair guidance, and documentation by analyzing device symptoms and user inputs to suggest probable issues and solutions. AI can also cross-reference specifications, generate step-by-step guides, search part databases, and automate maintenance scheduling.

Crafting Effective Prompts for Technician work

To maximize AI tool utility, technicians need precise prompts. This involves clearly stating the device type, observed symptoms, error codes, and part specifications. It helps to include model numbers, usage context, and past maintenance for repair requests. Detailed prompts yield accurate AI solutions for diagnosis, repair steps, or parts sourcing.

1. Troubleshooting Workflow Generation

Scenario

A technician needs an AI workflow for inconsistent desktop computer power failures to guide efficient troubleshooting.

> ***Prompt***
>
> *"You are assistant technician. Generate a detailed troubleshooting workflow for diagnosing the issue described below. Include sequential diagnostic steps, decision points, required tools, and likely root causes."*

How It Works

Using a tool like ChatGPT, Perplexity AI, or Gemini, first enter the prompt. Next, paste the device type, reported symptoms, and any preliminary checks from a text-based file (.txt, .docx) directly below it, and submit. The AI will generate a logical diagnostic path, ensuring a systematic and precise repair.

2. Root Cause Analysis for Recurring Faults

Scenario

A technician is troubleshooting a device that exhibits recurring faults even after multiple repairs. They need a root cause analysis to resolve the underlying issue.

> ***Prompt***
>
> *"You are a professional technician with 20 years experience in fault diagnosis and repairs. Analyze the following recurring fault in [specify device/model], considering its repair history and symptoms, and suggest the most probable root cause along with a permanent fix."*

How It Works

Using a tool like ChatGPT, Perplexity AI, or Gemini, first enter the prompt and ensure to specify the device model in the prompt entry. Next, paste the recurring fault symptoms, and previous repair attempts from a text-based file (.txt, .docx) directly below it, and submit. The AI will analyze the repair history and symptom patterns to isolate the root cause and recommend a permanent solution.

3. Fault Simulation for Training

Scenario

A senior technician is developing training materials for junior staff. They want AI to simulate a range of faults in a common device to aid instructional demonstrations.

> ***Prompt***
>
> *"You are a senior technician. Simulate realistic faults in [specify device name] to use in technician training. Include fault symptoms, probable causes, testing procedures, and expected diagnostic outcomes."*

How It Works

Using a tool like ChatGPT, Gemini, or Perplexity AI, first enter the prompt specifying the device name. Next, submit. The AI will simulate realistic faults, detailing symptoms, diagnostic procedures, probable causes, and corrective actions to support hands-on technician training.

4. Diagnostic Flowchart Generation

Scenario

A technician wants a visual diagnostic flowchart to streamline fault detection and resolution for a specific category of electronic devices.

> ***Prompt***
>
> *"You are a technician assistant. Create a diagnostic flowchart for the device and fault scenarios described below. The chart should cover input checks, common symptoms, test points, and recommended fixes."*

How It Works

Using a tool like ChatGPT, Perplexity AI, or Gemini, first enter the prompt. Next, paste the device category and common fault scenarios from a text-based file (.txt, .docx) directly below it, and submit. The AI will create a clear, logical diagnostic flowchart to assist technicians in rapid fault identification and precise resolution.

5. Spare Parts Compatibility and Sourcing

Scenario

A technician needs help identifying compatible spare parts for a faulty device and locating reliable sources for procurement.

> ***Prompt***
>
> *"You are a technician assistant expert in parts sourcing. List compatible spare parts for a [specify device/model] and suggest trusted sources or suppliers where they can be purchased, including part numbers and specifications."*

How It Works

Using a tool like Perplexity AI or Gemini, first enter the prompt specifying the device name or model. Next, paste the manufacturer, and component issue from a text-based file (.txt, .docx) directly below it, and submit. The AI will identify compatible spare parts based on technical data and suggest trusted suppliers, streamlining parts procurement.

6. Repair Cost Estimation and Quotation Drafting

Scenario

A technician is preparing a formal repair quotation for a client whose electrical device requires a control board replacement and rewiring.

> ***Prompt***
>
> *"You are a technician assistant responsible for invoicing. Generate a professional repair quotation for the device and issue described below. Include itemized parts, labor charges, estimated repair time, and a summary of the issue and solution."*

How It Works

Using a tool like ChatGPT, Microsoft Copilot, or Gemini, first enter the prompt. Next, paste the device type, diagnosed issue, part costs, and estimated labor hours from a text-based file (.txt, .docx) directly below it, and submit. The AI will generate a professional itemized quotation, enhancing client communication and transparency.

Conclusion

This chapter has demonstrated how large language models can be meaningfully integrated into the everyday realities of professional work. Through carefully designed, domain-specific prompt packs, prompt engineering is presented not as a purely technical exercise, but as a practical approach to improving clarity, precision, efficiency, and decision-making across diverse fields.

The scenarios throughout this chapter demonstrate how professionals can frame questions, structure information, and collaborate with AI systems to produce intelligent, relevant outputs. While the prompts provide practical starting points, their deeper purpose is to develop adaptive thinking, enabling readers to apply core prompting strategies such as role assignment, zero-shot, few-shot, and structured reasoning in ways that suit their own contexts.

As AI becomes embedded in more complex professional tasks, the ability to design clear, goal-oriented prompts will become increasingly essential. Prompting therefore stands not only as a future-ready skill, but as a present-day professional discipline, one that supports thoughtful judgment, responsible AI use, and more effective human-AI collaboration.

Glossary

AGI (Artificial General Intelligence)

A type of AI that possesses the ability to understand, learn, and apply knowledge across a wide range of tasks, matching or exceeding human intelligence. AGI remains a theoretical goal and has not yet been achieved.

AI Agent (Agentic AI)

An AI system capable of autonomous decision-making and task execution, often combining planning, reasoning, and memory. Unlike traditional models that respond only to prompts, agentic AI can pursue goals, adapt to feedback, and operate with minimal human supervision.

Algorithm

A step-by-step set of instructions or rules designed to perform a specific task or solve a problem. Algorithms form the backbone of AI systems and data processing.

Artificial Neural Networks (ANNs)

A machine learning architecture inspired by the human brain's network of neurons. ANNs are composed of interconnected nodes (neurons) and are widely used in deep learning tasks such as image recognition and language processing.

ASI (Artificial Superintelligence)

A hypothetical AI that surpasses human intelligence across all domains, including creativity, decision-making, and emotional intelligence. ASI remains speculative and poses philosophical and ethical questions.

Bias (in AI)

Systematic errors in AI models caused by skewed training data, flawed design, or cultural assumptions. Bias can lead to unfair outcomes and is a major concern in responsible AI development.

Big Data

Extremely large and complex datasets that require advanced technologies and methods for storage, analysis, and interpretation. Big data powers many AI applications, particularly predictive analytics.

Black Box (AI)

A term describing AI models whose internal decision-making processes are not easily interpretable by humans. Black-box systems raise challenges for trust, accountability, and transparency.

Blockchain

A decentralized digital ledger that records transactions across multiple computers securely and transparently. Increasingly relevant in AI for trust and verification.

Chain-of-Thought Prompting

An advanced prompting technique that guides AI to generate step-by-step reasoning when solving complex problems. It improves the model's ability to justify its responses.

Chatbot

An AI-driven conversational program that interacts with users through text or speech. Chatbots are widely used in customer service, education, and healthcare.

ChatGPT

A conversational AI developed by OpenAI, based on the GPT (Generative Pre-trained Transformer) architecture. It is widely used for drafting, coding, tutoring, and professional assistance.

Computer Vision

A field of AI that enables machines to interpret and process visual data such as images and video.

Applications include facial recognition, medical imaging, and autonomous vehicles.

COPPA (Children's Online Privacy Protection Act)

A U.S. law that regulates the online collection of personal data from children under 13. It impacts how AI systems must be designed for safety and compliance.

CPRA (California Privacy Rights Act)

An extension of the California Consumer Privacy Act (CCPA) that enhances consumer rights and introduces stricter compliance obligations for organizations using AI technologies.

Cross-Domain Learning

A machine learning technique where knowledge gained in one domain is applied to another. This enables models to adapt to new tasks with limited training data.

Cuebric AI

An AI tool for generating cinematic environments, widely used in creative storytelling, filmmaking, and virtual production.

Customer Segmentation (AI-enabled)

The use of machine learning to divide customers into groups based on behaviors or characteristics, enhancing personalization and marketing strategies.

DALL·E

A generative AI model by OpenAI that creates images from natural language descriptions, combining text understanding with computer vision.

Data Annotation

The process of labeling datasets (text, images, audio) for training AI models. High-quality annotation is critical for accuracy in supervised learning.

Data Ethics

The study and practice of responsible data collection, use, and sharing, ensuring fairness, accountability, and respect for privacy.

Data Mining

The process of discovering patterns, correlations, or anomalies in large datasets using AI and statistical techniques.

Data Preprocessing

The steps taken to clean, transform, and organize raw data before feeding it into a machine learning model. Preprocessing improves accuracy and model performance.

Data Privacy
The protection of personal and sensitive data in AI systems. It involves technical, legal, and ethical measures to ensure compliance with regulations such as the General Data Protection Regulation (GDPR) and the Health Insurance Portability and Accountability Act (HIPAA).

Deep Learning
A subset of machine learning that uses multi-layered artificial neural networks to learn complex patterns from data. Deep learning underpins applications such as image recognition, natural language processing, and autonomous driving.

DeepMind
An AI research company acquired by Google, known for breakthroughs in reinforcement learning and the development of AlphaGo, AlphaFold, and other advanced systems.

Digital Twin
A virtual model of a physical object, system, or process that is updated in real time. Used in manufacturing, engineering, and smart cities for monitoring and optimization.

Edge AI

AI processing that occurs locally on devices ("the edge") instead of centralized cloud servers. It enables faster decisions with lower latency and improved privacy, especially in IoT and robotics.

Ethical AI

An approach to AI development that prioritizes fairness, transparency, accountability, and alignment with human values. Ethical AI involves designing systems that avoid harm and respect social and legal norms.

Few-Shot Prompting

A prompting technique in which a language model is given a small number of examples to learn how to complete a task, helping it generalize without extensive fine-tuning.

Fine-Tuning

The process of further training a pre-trained model on a domain-specific dataset to improve accuracy and specialization.

Gemini

A family of large language models developed by Google DeepMind, designed for advanced reasoning and multimodal applications.

Generative AI (GenAI)

AI models capable of generating new content—such as text, images, music, or code—based on patterns learned from training data.

Generative Adversarial Networks (GANs)

A deep learning architecture with two competing networks: a generator that creates synthetic data and a discriminator that evaluates it. GANs are widely used in image synthesis and creative design.

GPU (Graphics Processing Unit)

A specialized processor optimized for parallel computing tasks, essential for training and running deep learning models.

GPT (Generative Pre-trained Transformer)

A family of large language models that generate human-like text based on prompts. GPT models are widely used for writing assistance, coding, and research.

Guardrails (in AI)

Design features or policies that constrain AI systems to operate safely and ethically, minimizing risks such as harmful outputs or misuse.

Hallucination (AI)

When an AI model generates content that is plausible but factually incorrect or fabricated. A known limitation of large language models.

Heuristics

Simplified, experience-based rules or strategies used to solve problems efficiently, though not always optimally.

HIPAA (Health Insurance Portability and Accountability Act)

A U.S. law that sets standards for protecting sensitive health information. AI systems in healthcare must comply with HIPAA requirements.

Humanoid Robot

A robot designed to resemble and mimic human appearance and behavior, often used in healthcare, education, and service industries.

Human-in-the-Loop (HITL)

A model of AI decision-making that requires human input, oversight, or approval at critical points, ensuring safety and accountability.

Inference (AI Inference)

The process by which an AI model generates predictions or decisions based on input data after training.

Image Recognition

An AI capability that identifies and classifies objects or patterns in digital images. It is central to computer vision.

Inpainting

A generative AI technique used to reconstruct or fill in missing parts of an image, applied in restoration and design.

InVideo AI

A generative AI platform that automates video creation from text prompts, scripts, or templates, widely used in media production.

Iterative Prompting

A method of refining outputs by repeatedly adjusting prompts based on prior responses, improving clarity and alignment.

JSON (JavaScript Object Notation)

A lightweight data-interchange format used for structuring and transmitting data between systems. Commonly used in AI APIs.

Knowledge Graph

A structured representation of entities and their relationships, enabling AI systems to reason and improve contextual understanding.

Large Language Model (LLM)

A machine learning model trained on massive text corpora to understand and generate human-like language. Examples include ChatGPT, Gemini, and Microsoft Copilot.

Leonardo AI

A generative AI platform for producing high-quality images and concept art, widely used in design and illustration.

LiDAR (Light Detection and Ranging)

A sensing technology that measures distances with laser pulses to generate 3D maps, often paired with AI for autonomous vehicles and robotics.

LLM-as-a-Service

A deployment model where large language models are offered as accessible cloud-based services.

Low-Code/No-Code AI

Platforms that enable users with limited technical expertise to create AI solutions through visual interfaces or pre-built modules.

Machine Learning (ML)

A branch of AI that enables systems to learn patterns from data and improve their performance without being explicitly programmed.

Meta-learning

"Learning to learn." A technique where models adapt quickly to new tasks with minimal training data.

Metadata

Information that describes data (such as file type, author, or date), aiding in organization, search, and interpretation.

Midjourney

A generative AI tool that produces high-quality images and artwork from text prompts.

Microsoft Copilot

An AI assistant integrated into Microsoft 365 applications, designed to enhance productivity by automating routine tasks.

Model Fine-tuning

The process of adapting a pre-trained AI model to perform better on a specific dataset or task.

Multimodal Learning

A machine learning approach that integrates multiple types of input—such as text, images, and audio—for richer contextual understanding.

Narrow AI

AI systems designed to perform specific tasks effectively but without broader reasoning or general intelligence.

Natural Language Processing (NLP)

A branch of AI that enables machines to understand, interpret, and generate human language. Applications include sentiment analysis, translation, and chatbots

Neural Networks

A computational model inspired by the human brain, consisting of interconnected nodes ("neurons") that process and transmit information. Neural networks underpin deep learning.

OECD AI Principles

Guidelines established by the Organisation for Economic Co-operation and Development promoting responsible AI aligned with fairness, transparency, and human-centered values.

OpenAI

An AI research and deployment organization known for developing models such as GPT, ChatGPT, and DALL·E.

Outpainting

A generative image technique where AI extends the boundaries of an image while maintaining visual coherence.

Parameters (Model Parameters)

The internal values learned by an AI model during training (such as weights and biases) that determine how the model processes input data to generate outputs.

Pattern Recognition

The ability of AI systems to identify regularities, trends, or structures within data. Pattern recognition underpins applications like handwriting analysis, speech recognition, and fraud detection.

Perplexity AI

A conversational AI and search tool that integrates real-time web data into responses with citations.

Predictive Analytics

The use of machine learning and statistical methods to forecast future outcomes based on historical data. It is applied in areas such as finance, healthcare, and marketing.

Prompt Chaining

A technique where the output of one prompt serves as the input for another, enabling multi-step workflows.

Prompt Engineering

The practice of designing and refining inputs (prompts) to guide AI models toward generating accurate, relevant, and high-quality outputs. It is a key skill in working effectively with large language models.

Prompt Injection

A vulnerability where malicious instructions are inserted into prompts to manipulate an AI system's behavior.

Publishing AI

AI systems and platforms that support publishing tasks, such as content creation, editing, and formatting.

Quantization

An optimization technique that reduces the precision of model parameters to improve efficiency without major accuracy loss.

Query Expansion

A method of improving search by adding related terms or synonyms to a user's original query.

Recurrent Neural Networks (RNNs)

A class of neural networks designed for sequential data such as text, speech, or time series.

Reinforcement Learning

A machine learning paradigm where agents learn by trial and error, guided by rewards and penalties.

Responsible AI

The practice of designing and deploying AI systems in alignment with ethical, legal, and societal standards.

Retrieval-Augmented Generation (RAG)

A hybrid AI approach that combines large language models with external knowledge retrieval, improving factual accuracy and reducing hallucinations.

Role Assignment (Prompting)

A prompting technique where the AI is instructed to "act as" a specific role (e.g., lawyer, developer, teacher) to improve relevance.

Robotics

The interdisciplinary field that combines AI with engineering to design machines capable of performing physical tasks autonomously.

Sentiment Analysis

A natural language processing task that identifies emotions, opinions, or attitudes expressed in text.

Supervised Learning

A machine learning approach that uses labeled data to train models for classification or prediction tasks.

Suno

An AI platform focused on generating music from text prompts using deep generative models. It allows users to create original soundtracks, jingles, and background music with minimal technical knowledge.

Tensor

A multi-dimensional numerical array used to represent data in deep learning frameworks.

TensorFlow

An open-source framework developed by Google for building and deploying AI models.

Token (in NLP)

A text unit—such as a word, character, or subword—used by language models to process and generate text.
Tokenization is the process of splitting text into tokens.

Training Data

The dataset used to teach machine learning models to recognize patterns and make predictions.

Transfer Learning

A method of reusing a pre-trained model's knowledge to improve performance on a new but related task.

Transparency (AI Transparency)

The practice of making AI models understandable and interpretable to build trust and accountability.

Turing Test

A benchmark proposed by Alan Turing to determine whether a machine's behavior is indistinguishable from that of a human.

TPU (Tensor Processing Unit)

A specialized processor developed by Google for accelerating deep learning tasks.

Unsupervised Learning

A machine learning method in which algorithms discover patterns in unlabeled data, often through clustering or dimensionality reduction.

User Intent

The underlying goal or purpose behind a user's query or prompt.

Utility Function

In reinforcement learning, a mathematical function that defines the goals of an agent by assigning values to different states or actions.

Vector Embeddings

Numerical representations of data in continuous vector space, capturing semantic meaning for tasks like search and recommendation.

Voice Cloning

The replication of a person's voice using AI to generate synthetic speech that closely mimics the original speaker.

Watson

IBM's AI platform for enterprise applications in healthcare, finance, and customer service.

XAI (Explainable AI)

A field of AI research focused on making models and decisions interpretable to humans.

XML (eXtensible Markup Language)
A markup language for structuring and exchanging data in human-readable and machine-readable formats.

YOLO (You Only Look Once)

A real-time object detection algorithm capable of identifying and classifying multiple objects within images or video in a single pass.

Zero-Shot Prompting

A prompting approach where a model performs a task without being provided examples, relying solely on prior training.

Zettelkasten
A knowledge management system based on linked note-taking, often integrated with AI-assisted research workflows.

Acknowledgment

Perfect Prompting owes its development and depth to the contributions of many individuals and institutions.

My sincere gratitude goes to the Microsoft and LinkedIn Learning instructors whose expert guidance on generative artificial intelligence, prompt engineering, and the evolution of intelligent search significantly informed this work. Having the opportunity to preview their instructional content was invaluable, and their thought leadership helped inspire the central question that frames this book: *How can we work intelligently with artificial intelligence?*

Special appreciation is extended to several thought leaders whose work provided important foundations:

- Pinar Seyhan Demirdag, generative AI expert and AI Director at Cuebric, for her pioneering insights into generative artificial intelligence.
- Ronnie Sheer, for his clear and practical instruction on prompt engineering principles.

- Ashley Kennedy, Managing Staff Instructor at LinkedIn Learning, Noelle Silver, award-winning technologist and Microsoft Most Valuable Professional in Artificial Intelligence, and Brandie Nonnecke, Founding Director of the CITRIS Policy Lab at the University of California, Berkeley, whose collective work on the evolution of thoughtful online search offered essential perspective on how reasoning systems are reshaping digital inquiry.

I also extend sincere appreciation to the developers and research teams behind the artificial intelligence tools that supported the creation of this book. ChatGPT and Perplexity assisted with early-stage research and draft development, while Gemini contributed to editing and clarity refinement. These tools not only enhanced the precision of the material but also demonstrate the growing potential of collaborative human and artificial intelligence creativity.

References

AI fundamentals: What is Artificial Intelligence

1. *Russell, S., & Norvig, P. (2020). Artificial Intelligence: A Modern Approach (4th ed.). Pearson.*
2. *Goodfellow, I., Bengio, Y., & Courville, A. (2016). Deep Learning. MIT Press.*
3. *Esteva, A., Kuprel, B., Novoa, R. A., Ko, J., Swetter, S. M., Blau, H. M., & Thrun, S. (2017). Dermatologist-level classification of skin cancer with deep neural networks. Nature, 542(7639), 115–118.*
4. *Mitchell, M. (2019). Artificial Intelligence: A Guide for Thinking Humans. Farrar, Straus and Giroux.*
5. *Nilsson, N. J. (2010). The Quest for Artificial Intelligence: A History of Ideas and Achievements. Cambridge University Press.*

Key elements of AI

1. *Mitchell, T. M. (1997). Machine Learning. McGraw-Hill.*
2. *Jurafsky, D., & Martin, J. H. (2023). Speech and Language Processing (3rd ed.). Pearson.*
3. *Szeliski, R. (2022). Computer Vision: Algorithms and Applications (2nd ed.). Springer.*
4. *Craig, J. J. (2005). Introduction to Robotics: Mechanics and Control (3rd ed.). Pearson.*

Types of AI

1. *.Nilsson, N. J. (2010). The Quest for Artificial Intelligence: A History of Ideas and Achievements. Cambridge University Press.*

2. *Russell, S. (2020). Human Compatible: Artificial Intelligence and the Problem of Control. Penguin Press.*
3. *Bostrom, N. (2014). Superintelligence: Paths, Dangers, Strategies. Oxford University Press.*
4. *Goertzel, B. & Pennachin, C. (2007). Artificial General Intelligence. Springer.*
5. *OpenAI. "GPT-4 Technical Report." OpenAI, 2023.*
6. *Tegmark, M. (2017). Life 3.0: Being Human in the Age of Artificial Intelligence. Knopf.*
7. *Yudkowsky, E. (2008). Artificial Intelligence as a Positive and Negative Factor in Global Risk. In Bostrom & Ćirković (Eds.), Global Catastrophic Risks. Oxford University Press.*

Narrow AI

1. *OpenAI. "GPT-4 Technical Report." OpenAI Research, 2023.*
2. *Anthropic. "Claude 2: A Safer LLM." Anthropic Research Blog, 2023.*
3. *Ricci, F., Rokach, L., & Shapira, B. (2015). Recommender Systems Handbook. Springer.*
4. *Garvie, C., Bedoya, A., & Frankle, J. (2016). The Perpetual Line-Up: Unregulated Police Face Recognition in America. Georgetown Law, Center on Privacy & Technology.*
5. *Jumper, J. et al. (2021). "Highly accurate protein structure prediction with AlphaFold." Nature, 596(7873), 583–589.*
6. *Aidoc. "AI Radiology Solutions." Accessed 2025. https://www.aidoc.com*
7. *Mastercard. "Decision Intelligence for Fraud Prevention." Mastercard Insights, 2022.*
8. *Hoy, M. B. (2018). "Alexa, Siri, Cortana, and More: An Introduction to Voice Assistants." Medical Reference Services Quarterly, 37(1), 81–88.*

Transforming Industries with AI

1. *McKinsey Global Institute. (2018). AI Adoption Advances, but Foundational Barriers Remain.*
2. *Esteva, A., et al. (2017). Dermatologist-level classification of skin cancer with deep neural networks. Nature, 542(7639), 115–118.*
3. *Arner, D. W., Barberis, J., & Buckley, R. P. (2016). The evolution of Fintech: A new post-crisis paradigm. Georgetown Journal of International Law, 47, 1271–1319.*
4. *Holmes, W., Bialik, M., & Fadel, C. (2019). Artificial Intelligence in Education: Promises and Implications for Teaching and Learning. Center for Curriculum Redesign.*
5. *Lee, J., et al. (2015). Predictive Manufacturing System—Trends of Next-Generation Production Systems. Procedia CIRP, 33, 233–238.*
6. *Grewal, D., et al. (2020). The future of retailing. Journal of Retailing, 96(1), 69–89.*
7. *Litman, T. (2020). Autonomous vehicle implementation predictions. Victoria Transport Policy Institute.*
8. *Seaver, N. (2019). Captivating algorithms: Recommender systems as traps. Journal of Material Culture, 24(4), 421–436.*

Ethical and Societal Challenges in AI

1. *Buolamwini, J., & Gebru, T. (2018). Gender shades: Intersectional accuracy disparities in commercial gender classification. Proceedings of Machine Learning Research, 81, 1–15.*
2. *Zuboff, S. (2019). The Age of Surveillance Capitalism. PublicAffairs.*
3. *Rudin, C. (2019). Stop explaining black box machine learning models for high-stakes decisions and use interpretable models instead. Nature Machine Intelligence, 1(5), 206–215.*
4. *Brynjolfsson, E., & McAfee, A. (2014). The Second Machine Age. W. W. Norton & Company.*
5. *Calo, R. (2015). Robotics and the lessons of cyberlaw. California Law Review, 103(3), 513–563.*

6. *Taylor, L., Floridi, L., & Van der Sloot, B. (Eds.). (2017). Group Privacy: New Challenges of Data Technologies. Springer.*
7. *European Commission. (2021). Proposal for a Regulation Laying Down Harmonised Rules on Artificial Intelligence (Artificial Intelligence Act). Brussels.*
8. *Bostrom, N. (2014). Superintelligence: Paths, Dangers, Strategies. Oxford University Press*

How AI Works

1. *Domingos, P. (2015). The Master Algorithm: How the Quest for the Ultimate Learning Machine Will Remake Our World. Basic Books.*
2. *LeCun, Y., Bengio, Y., & Hinton, G. (2015). Deep learning. Nature, 521(7553), 436–444.*
3. *Mitchell, T. M. (1997). Machine Learning. McGraw-Hill.*
4. *Goodfellow, I., Bengio, Y., & Courville, A. (2016). Deep Learning. MIT Press.*
5. *Vaswani, A., et al. (2017). Attention is all you need. Advances in Neural Information Processing Systems, 30.*
6. *OpenAI. (2023). GPT-4 Technical Report. https://openai.com/research/gpt-4*
7. *Marcus, G. (2022). Deep learning is hitting a wall. MIT Technology Review. https://www.technologyreview.com*

What is Prompt Engineering

1. *Reynolds, L., & McDonell, K. (2021). Prompt Programming for Large Language Models: Beyond the Few-Shot Paradigm. arXiv preprint arXiv:2102.07350.*
2. *Brown, T. B., et al. (2020). Language models are few-shot learners. Advances in Neural Information Processing Systems, 33, 1877–1901.*
3. *Surden, H. (2014). Machine Learning and Law. Washington Law Review, 89(1), 87–115.*
4. *Holmes, W., Bialik, M., & Fadel, C. (2019). Artificial Intelligence in Education: Promises and Implications for Teaching and Learning. Center for Curriculum Redesign.*

5. *Esteva, A., et al. (2019). A guide to deep learning in healthcare. Nature Medicine, 25(1), 24–29.*
6. *Chui, M., et al. (2018). Notes from the AI frontier: Applications and value of deep learning. McKinsey Global Institute Discussion Paper.*
7. *Pearce, H., et al. (2023). Asleep at the Keyboard? Assessing the Security of GitHub Copilot's Code Contributions. IEEE Symposium on Security and Privacy.*
8. *Weidinger, L., et al. (2022). Ethical and social risks of harm from language models. Proceedings of the 2022 ACM Conference on Fairness, Accountability, and Transparency.*

Advanced Prompting Techniques

1. *Brown, T. B., et al. (2020). Language models are few-shot learners. Advances in Neural Information Processing Systems, 33, 1877–1901.*
2. *Kojima, T., et al. (2022). Large Language Models are Zero-Shot Reasoners. arXiv preprint arXiv:2205.11916.*
3. *Wei, J., et al. (2022). Chain-of-thought prompting elicits reasoning in large language models. arXiv preprint arXiv:2201.11903.*
4. *OpenAI. (2023). GPT-4 Technical Report. Retrieved from https://openai.com/research/gpt-4*
5. *Reimers, N., & Gurevych, I. (2020). Making Monolingual Sentence Embeddings Multilingual using Knowledge Distillation. Proceedings of the 2020 Conference on Empirical Methods in Natural Language Processing (EMNLP).*

AI Tools and Their Effective Use Cases

Openai (2025) https://openai.com/research/gpt-4

Google DeepMind (2025). https://deepmind.google/technologies/gemini
Perplexity AI (2025). https://www.perplexity.ai
Microsoft (2025). https://www.microsoft.com/copilot
Suno (2025). https://www.suno.com
Midjourney (2025). https://www.midjourney.com
Canva (2025). Magic Studio & Visual Suite 2.0 Features (canva.com)

Leonardo AI (2025). Phoenix & Creative Suite leonardo.ai (fahimai.com, youtube.com)
Cuebric & Disguise partnership (2023–2025)(disguise.one). (livedesignonline.com)
InVideo (2025). (help.invideo.io).

Limitations of AI

1. *Bender, E. M., Gebru, T., McMillan-Major, A., & Shmitchell, S. (2021). On the Dangers of Stochastic*
2. *Parrots: Can Language Models Be Too Big? Proceedings of the 2021 ACM Conference on Fairness, Accountability, and Transparency.*
3. *OpenAI (2024). GPT-4 Technical Report. https://openai.com/research/gpt-4*
4. *Anthropic (2024). Claude 3 System Card. https://www.anthropic.com/index/claude-3*
5. *Google DeepMind (2024). Gemini Technical Overview. https://deepmind.google/technologies/gemini*
6. *European Commission (2024). AI Act: Regulation on Artificial Intelligence. https://artificialintelligenceact.eu*
7. *EPI (2023). AI Hallucinations and Misinformation Risks. Ethics and Policy Initiative.*

AI Regulations and Compliance

1. OECD. (2019). *Recommendation of the Council on Artificial Intelligence.* OECD Legal Instruments. https://legalinstruments.oecd.org/en/instruments/OECD-LEGAL-0449
2. UNESCO. (2021). *Recommendation on the Ethics of Artificial Intelligence.* UNESCO Digital Library. https://unesdoc.unesco.org/ark:/48223/pf0000381115
3. European Commission. (2026). *Digital Omnibus Package: Proposed Amendments to Regulation (EU) 2024/1689 (Artificial Intelligence Act).*
4. European Union. (2016). *Regulation (EU) 2016/679 (General Data*

Protection Regulation).

5. U.S. Department of Justice. (2026, January 9). *Memorandum on the Creation of the Artificial Intelligence Litigation Task Force.*
6. California State Legislature. (2025). *Senate Bill No. 53: Transparency in Frontier Artificial Intelligence Act.*
7. California State Legislature. (2018). *California Consumer Privacy Act of 2018 (CCPA).*
8. Colorado General Assembly. (2024). *Senate Bill 24-205: Concerning Consumer Protections in Interactions with Artificial Intelligence Systems.*
9. Federal Trade Commission. (1998). *Children's Online Privacy Protection Act (COPPA).* 15 U.S.C. §§ 6501-6506.
10. Government of Canada. (2000). *Personal Information Protection and Electronic Documents Act (PIPEDA).* S.C. 2000, c. 5.
11. Treasury Board of Canada Secretariat. (2024). *Directive on Automated Decision-Making.* Government of Canada.
12. UK Government. (2018). *Data Protection Act 2018.*
13. Australian Government. (1988). *Privacy Act 1988.*
14. National Assembly of the Republic of Korea. (2025). *Framework Act on the Development of Artificial Intelligence and Establishment of Trust (AI Basic Act).* Act No. 20410.

About the Author

Eric Agyemang Duah is a generative AI specialist, author, trainer, and consultant who helps professionals and organizations apply AI in practical, ethical, and results-driven ways. He delivers generative AI training for individuals and corporate institutions, equipping teams with the skills to integrate AI into real-world workflows. His work focuses on turning complex AI capabilities into clear, actionable strategies that improve productivity, strengthen decision-making, and spark innovation across industries. By bridging technical knowledge with practical application, Eric empowers people to work more intelligently with AI.

Connect with Eric: **linkedin.com/in/prompttech**

Index

www.ingramcontent.com/pod-product-compliance
Lightning Source LLC
La Vergne TN
LVHW090300210926
848480LV00001B/82